The Essential Hybrid Car Handbook

The Essential Hybrid Car Handbook
{A Buyer's Guide}

Nick Yost

Foreword by David Friedman,
Union of Concerned Scientists

The Lyons Press
Guilford, Connecticut
An Imprint of The Globe Pequot Press

10 9 8 7 6 5 4 3 2 1

Printed in the United States of America
Designed by Georgiana Goodwin
Illustrations on pages 30–35 by Mary Balachino

Library of Congress Cataloging-in-Publication Data

Yost, Nick.
  The essential hybrid car handbook : a buyer's guide / Nick Yost.
      p. cm.
  Includes index.
  ISBN-13: 978-1-59921-019-3
  ISBN-10: 1-59921-019-3
  1. Hybrid electric cars—Purchasing. 2. Alternative fuel vehicles—Purchasing.
  3. Automobiles—Fuel consumption. I. Title.
  TL221.15.Y67 2006
  629.22'93—dc22
                        2006022142

✿ To Debora, the electricity in my life

{Contents}

03:

Future Hybrids, Alternative-Fuel Vehicles, and Super-efficient Small Cars | 93

x

You should read this book. And if you can afford it, you should buy a clean, high fuel economy hybrid. If you can't do that, you should choose the highest fuel economy car or truck that meets your needs.

Why? Because you want to spend less money on gas. Because you support the U.S. auto industry. Because you care about your future and the future of your children and their children. Because you are a patriot.

Or, perhaps, because you think hybrids are cool, and you just have to have one. Either way, purchasing a hybrid that goes farther on a gallon of gas or just a conventional high fuel economy car or truck can be one of the best decisions you make as a consumer.

America is addicted to oil. Our forty-third president said it and we all know it. Our oil addiction is a burden on our economy and our foreign policy. We import over 60 percent of our oil and other petroleum products. With oil at $60 per barrel, every minute that passes takes with it more than $500,000 that could have been spent creating U.S. jobs and strengthening our economy. Instead, that money supports our oil habit.

Every major oil price shock since the 1970s has been linked to rising inflation and recession. Today's economy, while more resilient to higher oil prices than in the past, is still quite vulnerable. Continued political instability in many major oil-producing nations, some of which are not exactly our allies, constantly threatens to create new oil price shocks.

If you care about America's economy, American jobs, our international standing, and foreign policy, then you care about our oil addiction. And one of the fastest and most effective ways to tackle that problem is to drive cars that get more miles to the gallon, whether they are high fuel economy hybrids or other high fuel economy cars and trucks.

But high fuel economy and hybrids aren't just about concern for the country; they are also about protecting your pocketbook. The average car owner's budget shrinks by more than $280 per year when gasoline jumps from about $1.50 per gallon to $2.00 per gallon, roughly what happened to American consumers between 2003 and 2004. Gasoline prices at $3.00 per gallon shrink the average budget by more than $850 per year, compared to gasoline at half that price.

With gasoline price premiums of more than $800, it does not take long for fuel savings from higher fuel economy vehicles to cover their added up-front cost. This is especially true when you consider the fact that the average new vehicle sold today gets worse fuel economy than it did twenty years ago, according to the U.S. Environmental Protection Agency. Some hybrids today will pay back their added cost in the first five years; others will take longer. But in a world of $3.00 per gallon of gasoline, you shouldn't have too much of a problem convincing the next owner to pay a bit extra for a patriotic gas sipper. And if you hold on to your hybrid and maintain it well, it will be a great investment.

Of course, the cost of our oil addiction does not end at just our own bank accounts. High oil consumption leads to high gasoline prices, which represent one of the single largest threats facing automaker jobs in America. A recent study led by the University of Michigan[1] shows that sustained high gasoline prices around $3.00 per gallon would put 300,000 American autoworkers out of their jobs by the end of this decade. When gas prices go up, people simply have less money to spend on buying new vehicles.

On the other hand, increased fuel economy represents a significant opportunity not only to protect, but also to increase the number of autoworker jobs in America. Analysis by the Union of Concerned Scientists[2] indicates that increasing fuel economy could create as many as 160,000 new jobs nationwide over the next decade, with 40,000 in the auto industry alone. These jobs come from consumers spending less on gasoline and more on new cars and other products throughout the economy. So if you want to support auto industry jobs in America, sending the signal that you want more miles per gallon is clearly the way to go.

Higher fuel economy is also a key ingredient necessary to tackle global warming, the biggest long-term environmental threat facing our country and the world. Only the entire economies of the United States, China, and Russia exceed the carbon dioxide being emitted by U.S. cars and trucks alone. That carbon dioxide is the primary gas wrapping the Earth in a continually thickening heat-trapping blanket.

We are already seeing the impact that our cars and other sources of global warming pollution are having on the Earth. Nineteen of the twenty hottest years on record have occurred since 1980, and 2006 is on track to break the record. As the Earth continues to warm, we face a great risk that the climate will change in ways that threaten not only our health and the economy, but our farms, forests, beaches, wetlands, and other natural habitats as well.

[1] Walter S. McManus et al. *In the Tank: How Oil Prices Threaten Automakers' Profits and Jobs,* University of Michigan Transportation Research Institute, July 2005.

[2] David J. Friedman et al. *Creating Jobs, Saving Energy and Protecting the Environment: An Analysis of the Potential Benefits of Investing in Efficient Cars and Trucks,* Union of Concerned Scientists, July 2004.

As with our economic vulnerability, our climate vulnerability can be addressed in part by cutting back on the amount of oil we use. At today's low average of 21 mpg for a new vehicle, about one pound of global warming pollution comes out of the tailpipe for every mile you drive. Another quarter-pound is produced from making and shipping the gasoline. On the other hand, a hybrid boosts fuel economy by 50 percent and can cut that by one-third—not bad for a vehicle that also creates jobs and saves money at the gas pump.

Of course, at the end of the day, some might have yet another reason to buy a high fuel economy hybrid—because they are cool cars and trucks. The good ones have the latest technology and help you stand out in a crowd. If that is your reason for buying one and you make sure part of that purchase is high fuel economy, then great, because all the other benefits will come along as well.

There are many reasons to put fuel economy at or near the top of your car-buying list, but shopping for a car or truck is never that easy. Hybrids expand your choices in the marketplace, and this book can help you sort through the alternatives to find the best hybrid or high fuel economy vehicle for you. Remember, hybrids are not created equal, so whether you want to focus on the highest fuel economy hybrids or find a compromise between luxury and fuel economy, don't just believe the marketing hype about any particular vehicle. Instead, do your research and make sure to compare the fuel economy, emissions, and the costs of the options out there.

Here is my advice: read this book, check out some of the resources available on the Web, and then choose the highest fuel economy car or truck that meets your needs. Although we must continue to tap into alternative fuels, find ways to drive less, and get even better fuel economy technology on the market, your decision can make an important contribution to cutting our oil addiction. Not only that, but you will feel good about the purchase because you will be getting better technology, doing your part to tackle global warming, supporting American jobs, and protecting your pocketbook. Plus, I am not sure that buying a gas guzzler will make you feel too patriotic.

David J. Friedman
Research Director
Clean Vehicles
Union of Concerned Scientists
August 2006

When I began work on this book, I believed that I was familiar with hybrid cars and had a basic understanding of how they work. I was naïve enough to think that the hybrid powerplants developed by Toyota, Honda, and Ford pretty much covered the territory.

It didn't take me long to realize that hybrid technology is expanding, becoming more versatile, and growing more efficient. With the arrival of $3-a-gallon gasoline, it's clear that the automotive industry can no longer operate on the assumption that an inexpensive, nearly limitless supply of fuel will be available to get our goods, our services, and ourselves where we need to be.

It's time to look elsewhere, to seek new solutions. The good news is that the automotive industry, the scientific community, and the government are all working hard to make change happen. Hybrid vehicles, which use self-generated, pollution-free electrical power to reduce fossil fuel consumption, are an important first step toward energy independence. They are not perfect, but their benefits clearly outweigh their liabilities.

On the downside, hybrid powerplants are more expensive to produce than conventional engines. The price differential may diminish, but it will probably never disappear. Hybrids do not deliver the fuel mileage estimated by the Environmental Protection Agency's unrealistic testing techniques. Hybrid vehicles will be compromised by bulky, space-robbing battery packs until electrical storage devices are developed that are substantially smaller, cheaper, and more powerful. That could be soon—or it could be years away.

But those negatives pale when weighed against the substantial benefits.

Hybrid vehicles are convenient. You hop in and simply drive away, just as you would in a conventional car or truck. You can fill up the tank at any one of the 180,000 gas stations operating across the country. The service intervals for hybrids are similar to those for conventional vehicles. Hybrids have proven to be reliable, and their battery packs can last for the life of the car.

Hybrid vehicles are fuel sippers. Despite the disappointment engendered by the EPA consumption figures, hybrid powerplants deliver much better fuel mileage than similarly powered gasoline engines.

Hybrid vehicles are clean. The less gasoline a vehicle burns, the less it pollutes.

Hybrid vehicles are not as expensive as many people think. The cost differential is already disappearing for some buyers, thanks to tax credits and private industry incentives for employees or customers.

Hybrid vehicles are not choosy. Ethanol, biodiesel, gasoline, diesel fuel: the hybrid vehicle doesn't care. Gasoline is the only choice now, but any fuel that works in an internal combustion engine could be part of a hybrid powerplant.

Hybrid vehicles have already improved significantly. Toyota is in its third generation of hybrid technology and Honda is in its second. Their current hybrid vehicles are more powerful and more fuel efficient than the originals.

Toyota announces its advanced technology on every hybrid vehicle.

All of that is just for starters. The future is bright with the promise of even more efficient and cleaner hybrid systems. Right now, better batteries are the key.

Intense development is under way to replace today's nickel-metal hydride batteries with the more compact and more powerful lithium-ion batteries. Lithium-ion batteries already work well in laptop computers and iPods, but battery producers and automotive manufacturers must be sure that bigger, stronger versions will be safe and reliable for the life of hybrid vehicles.

When that happens, hybrids will be able to travel much farther on electrical power alone. The future may also include the ultracapacitor, a device that can capture and release large amounts of electrical energy quickly. In a hybrid vehicle, it could gather electricity during braking, then release it during acceleration.

At the same time, engineers are working to reduce the emissions and increase the efficiency of gasoline and diesel engines while additional researchers are busy trying to perfect methods of producing alternate fuels that could replace oil.

Also on the horizon are modified hybrid vehicles, known as plug-ins, which can run much greater distances on electrical power alone and be recharged overnight at home. The technology is already in place, but without mass production quantities it could add as much as $10,000 to the price of the vehicle. Lithium-ion batteries and a lower price point could make plug-ins practical for the average car buyer. This would mean a motorist's daily commute or around-town errands could be made on electrical power alone.

The California Cars Initiative—a group that champions efficient, nonpolluting automotive technologies—has already adapted a Toyota Prius with a nickel-metal hydride battery to take a charge from a conventional 120-volt home outlet. The organization has received positive feedback from President George W. Bush and other influential politicians and businessmen. Japanese giant Toyota is working on the development of its own plug-in technology and so, reportedly, is General Motors.

General Motors, DaimlerChrysler, and BMW recently announced a joint effort to produce a two-mode hybrid system that employs electric motors inside the transmission. It can be adapted for use in everything from small cars to big sport-utility vehicles. A similar system is already in use in General Motors buses.

Meanwhile, the Environmental Protection Agency has obtained a patent for a hydraulic hybrid system. It uses hydraulic pressure to capture energy lost in braking, then releases the pressure during acceleration. The EPA estimates it could improve fuel efficiency by as much as 55%, at a cost to the consumer of about $1,000. Pilot projects are being conducted with Ford Motor Co., the U.S. Army, Eaton Corp., and United Parcel Service. If it proves to be feasible, the hydraulic hybrid system might work best in heavy-duty vehicles, such as garbage trucks, that accelerate and brake a lot over short distances. Other projects are under way at companies big and small: it remains to be seen what solutions will be the most practical.

I don't know when, or even if, hybrid power will become popular enough to be considered mainstream. It will take many solutions—hybrids, alternative fuels, more efficient gasoline and diesel engines, lighter and more aerodynamic vehicles—to wean us away from what President Bush calls America's addiction to oil. But my research has taught me one thing, voiced by David Friedman, research director for the Union of Concerned Scientists, during a talk to a group of automotive journalists: "There is no silver bullet—no one answer."

For now, however, the hybrid vehicle is the best answer we've got. It is here. It works. It is efficient. It is clean. And it is getting better.

When the Lexus LS600h goes on sale next year, it will tell its owners when its hybrid powertrain is available for duty.

01:
{Is a Hybrid Car for You?}

The sleek Honda Insight is designed
to cut through the wind.

{Is a Hybrid Car for You?}

Getting to Know a New Kind of Vehicle

You want a new car. You need a new car. You're going to get a new car—but what? Something fun? Something practical? Something fun and practical? Something politically correct? Picking out that new set of wheels has always been a delicate balancing act, but making the right decision has never been more difficult than it is today. Soaring gasoline prices, dwindling petroleum reserves, air pollution, safety equipment: they all come into play.

To make that decision even more complicated, along come the hybrid cars and trucks. Are they any good? How do they work? Are they easy to drive? Do they really get great gas mileage? Will they reduce smog? Are they worth the money? Will they work for my family? Are they any fun? The answers to these questions, along with a lot more information about what's happening in today's rapidly changing automotive industry, will be found in the pages of this handy guide.

In a nutshell, hybrid cars combine a conventional internal combustion engine with an electric motor to supply a vehicle's power. The assist from the electric motor gives a small engine the ability to perform like a more powerful one. The result is reduced fuel consumption and less air polution. Let's start by taking a look at how these new vehicles got a toehold in the U.S. market and how well they performed for the early adopters who embraced them.

Honda Insight: Got There First

When Japanese manufacturer Honda introduced its Insight to the American motorist in December of 1999, it also ushered in a radically different concept in modern automotive transportation: the hybrid car. The tiny two-seater was powered by a 1-liter, three-cylinder engine that worked in combination with an electric motor.

The partnership resulted in only 67 horsepower, but that was enough to move the Insight safely on U.S. roads, to propel it easily to extra-legal speeds, and to return, under ideal circumstances, an unheard-of 70 miles per gallon of

ordinary gasoline. Equally important, it belched fewer pollutants into the air than any other production car on the road.

This late-twentieth-century marketing of hybrid power was greeted with a combination of fascination and skepticism. The technically curious and environmentally concerned embraced it warmly, but others viewed the Insight as a mere curiosity, a toy of such limited practicality that it would soon be relegated to the trash bin of failed automotive oddities. Only seventeen Insights rolled out of the showroom that first month.

Nevertheless, a star was born. A few months later the Honda Insight was chosen as the pace car for the 2000 Tour de Sol, an annual showcase of the country's cleanest and most fuel-efficient cars, trucks, and buses. A group of owner-driven Insights also participated in the 292-mile run between New York City and Washington, D.C. The pace car used only 3.5 gallons of gasoline for an average of 83.6 miles per gallon. It came in first in the division for mass-produced cars. Another Insight, competing in the same division, won top honors for best mileage in a single measured portion of the journey. It averaged 94 miles per gallon over 68 miles.

Of course, with room for only two and little more than a handful of luggage, the Insight never sold in numbers greater than a few hundred or, at most, a few thousand a year. With only a few hundred sold in the first four months of 2006, Honda announced it was dropping production of the Insight. But, the company promised to introduce an all-new, relatively inexpensive hybrid car in 2009. Nevertheless, the Insight remains the fuel efficiency leader—a showcase of Honda know-how and proof that hybrid power can be a viable alternative to the traditional powerplants.

The Insight has also given rise to a cult-like band of owners, most of them enthralled by the technology, who take great pleasure in extracting the maximum amount of mileage from each gallon of fuel—and then telling fellow owners and everyone else how they did it. Their raves are sprinkled throughout hybrid car Internet Web sites that are frequented by fellow owner-enthusiasts.

Hypermilers

Hypermilers are the hybrid super-enthusiasts—the owners who do everything they can to exceed the Environmental Protection Agency's estimates of a vehicle's fuel mileage.

Although he rejects the hypermiler label, Bob Wilson, an engineer from Huntsville, Alabama, is a good example of one. He has been averaging 49.1 miles per gallon in his 2003 Toyota Prius since he bought it in October of 2005. That beats the EPA estimate of 48 mpg.

He is always thinking how he can squeeze a little more distance out of every gallon. He shuts the car down at red lights and plots routes that maximize use of the electric motor alone. He measures his car's efficiency at different speeds, in hot and cold weather.

He offers these tips to other hybrid owners:

1. Keep tire pressure well above the manufacturer's recommendation, to lower rolling resistance.
2. Do not fill the oil reservoir to the full mark. That reduces the power needed to keep the oil circulating.
3. Don't speed.
4. On the open road, find a tractor-trailer cruising at the speed limit and tuck in a safe distance behind it. This will lower your car's wind resistance.
5. Do not exceed 25 mph until the engine warms up. The gasoline engine will not shut off until it is warmed up.

Here are a few more tips from other hypermilers:

1. Remove all excess weight from the vehicle.
2. Step on the accelerator as if there were a raw egg under it.
3. Keep the car properly tuned for maximum efficiency.

The hybrid vehicle may seem to be an invention of the 1990s, but its origin actually goes all the way back to the 1890s. Various manufacturers produced cars and trucks powered by gasoline and electricity until about 1920. The most notable among the hybrid developers was one of the earliest: Ferdinand Porsche, father of the Volkswagen. Here is how he and the other manufacturers fit into the hybrid picture.

1900. Porsche introduces the System Lohner-Porsche electric carriage, powered by two Porsche-designed electric motors attached to the front wheels. It can exceed 35 miles per hour, but its batteries can not store enough electricity to provide long-range cruising. Porsche later overcomes this with his System Mixte. An onboard internal combustion engine powers a generator that supplies electricity to the wheel-mounted motors.

Meanwhile, the Belgium company Pieper produces a vehicle with a 3½-horsepower gasoline engine and an electric motor mounted under the seat. When the car coasts, the electric motor acts as a generator to charge the batteries. When needed, the electric motor gives the gasoline engine a power boost. (In concept, it is very similar to the hybrid system used today in Honda hybrid automobiles).

1903. Porsche builds a car with electric motors at all four wheels. It can hit 70 miles per hour. Krieger, a French company, produces a car that uses a gasoline engine to supplement a battery pack. It also features front-wheel drive and power steering.

1905. Porsche is awarded the Poetting prize, which honors him as Austria's outstanding engineer.

1910. A hybrid truck that uses a four-cylinder engine to power a generator is introduced, eliminating the need for batteries or a transmission. The truck is produced in Philadelphia until 1918.

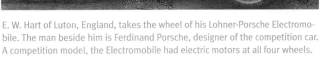
E. W. Hart of Luton, England, takes the wheel of his Lohner-Porsche Electromobile. The man beside him is Ferdinand Porsche, designer of the competition car. A competition model, the Electromobile had electric motors at all four wheels.

1914. The Galt Motor Company of Ontario, Canada, produces a hybrid with a two-cylinder, 10-horsepower engine driving a 40-volt, 90-ampere motor. The company claims the car can get 70 miles per gallon of gas, but its top speed of 30 miles per hour is not competitive with other vehicles.

1917. Woods Dual Power of Chicago produces a vehicle that uses a gasoline engine and electric motors working in tandem.

1920: By about 1920, with gasoline engines rapidly advancing in power and sophistication, the hybrid powerplant (engine and motor) is no longer competitive and disappears as a viable source of automotive power. In the United States, several attempts are made to produce all-electric and

Woods Dual Power car.

hybrid vehicles between 1965 and 1990, but none of the results are deemed worthy of mass production. Toyota reignites the hybrid flame with its Prius, introduced in Japan in 1997.

What the Owners Say: Honda Insight

It's not the car for everybody, of course, but the Honda Insight has proven to be a very satisfying automobile for the thousands of people who have bought them. Owners are impressed with the reliability, the longevity, the fun-to-drive factor, and, of course, the fuel savings and the reduced pollution. The occasional dissatisfied customer complains about the lack of luggage space and the car's buffeting by crosswinds and tractor-trailer trucks.

"My wife, son, and I all have been driving Honda Insights since 2000. We have a combined 170,000-plus miles. In the beginning, wow! Silent, fast, comfortable, super handling . . . trips with 60, 70, 80 miles per gallon, one 740-mile fill-up . . . We rarely calculate the gas savings, although we are proud of having bought over 2,800 less gallons of gas in a time when oil has caused so much trouble for so many people." That enthusiast calls himself Insight Owner about No. 4000.

Another enthusiast, Lynn C. of Virginia, reports: "We bought a Honda Insight about a year ago and love it. We regularly get 65 to 67 miles per gallon and occasionally get up to 75 . . . The best thing about our Insight is that we know we are having the least environmental impact possible when we drive."

Chuck, a Texan, is another Insight devotee. "I bought my 2000 Insight September 7, 2000. Five and a half years later and nearly 95,000 miles later, I've had the best experience of the seven cars I've owned—four of them Hondas . . . My lifetime miles per gallon is 57.5, but over the last year it's about 70. Unless it's a very short drive, you have to work to get the miles per gallon under 50."

Toyota Prius: Also a First

Although most Americans didn't realize it at the time, Honda was neither the first nor the only manufacturer in recent history to see the possibilities of hybrid power. Japanese giant Toyota had been selling its hybrid Prius in Japan since 1997 and was quick to follow Honda to American shores.

The Prius' burgeoning success is a story of commitment, patience, hard work, and setbacks that was chronicled in a *Fortune* magazine story by journalist Alex Taylor. It stretches all the way back to 1993, when Eiji Toyoda, chairman of the Japanese auto giant, let it be known that he had concerns about the future of the automobile. It was the signal the research and development staff needed to begin development of an automobile that could be sold worldwide in the twenty-first century.

Initially, the goal for the project, known as G21, was simply to build a vehicle that would get 47.5 miles per gallon, 50% more than the Toyota Corolla. Shortly thereafter, with twenty-first-century, middle-class families in mind, the developers decided it would also have to be roomier.

To this point, there was no specific plan for G21—and certainly no thought of hybrid power. However, the concept was not new. Toyota had been experimenting with gas-electric powerplants for a generation and work had been under way

Did You Hear the One About . . .

One of the most enduring legends in automotive lore is about the 200-mile-per-gallon carburetor. It apparently all started with Charles Nelson Pogue.

A Canadian inventor, Pogue sought patents between 1928 and 1936 for a new carburetor that would greatly reduce fuel usage. When word of his invention got out, stories circulated about cars with Pogue carburetors getting more than 200 miles per gallon. The manager of a Winnipeg car dealership claimed 217 miles on a single gallon of gasoline. A Canadian magazine told of a 1,879-mile journey on 14.5 gallons of gas; Pogue denied it, but the stories kept coming.

Eventually, the skeptics challenged Pogue's device but were never given permission to see the carburetor. As a result, Pogue and talk of his supposed invention simply faded away.

But the stories continued, only with a different twist. There was one about the General Motors retiree who returned his car to the factory to learn about his amazing gas mileage. The mechanic checked it out and returned the car. It ran fine, but the mileage was back to normal.

Other stories have circulated about high-fuel-mileage cars being bought back by the manufacturer for huge sums, of thieves stealing them, even of the government spiriting away a magnificent mileage maker. But they never make it past a reality check.

As the editors at www.snopes .com, a Web site devoted to debunking urban myths, asked: "Why would the manufacturer of a car, or a carburetor, keep it away from consumers? An automaker's self interest is best served by getting the newest irresistible technology to the consumer before his competitors do."

on a hybrid minivan. That project sputtered in a dispute between the engineers, who believed hybrid power would assure long-term viability of the automobile, and sales executives, who felt production costs would make it too expensive to be commercially successful.

The initial plan for G21 in 1994 was for an improved engine and transmission that would meet the fuel efficiency goal. But it was rejected by executive vice president Akihiro Wada on the grounds that G21 had to be something more than just another fuel-efficient Japanese compact car.

Wada had something else in mind: hybrid power. He ordered the development team to produce a hybrid concept car in time for the 1995 Tokyo Motor Show, a mere year away. And he wanted 100% improvement in fuel efficiency.

The team filtered through eighty hybrid combinations, dealing with a multiplicity of problems. It made its final choice in June of 1995 and set December 1998 as the target date for production of the automobile, which was by then known as the Prius.

A couple of months later, to the dismay of team members, the production date was moved up one full year by Hiroshi Okuda, who had become company president. This left only twenty-four months until production, about two-thirds the time required for development of a traditionally powered car.

Again, problems bedeviled the effort, but no less than a thousand engineers assigned to the project worked them out, one by one. Finally, the car achieved

This is the first Toyota Prius to be introduced in the United States. The gas-electric hybrid sedan arrived in July of 2000.

its goal of 66 miles per gallon. The Prius was introduced in Japan in October of 1997, two months ahead of schedule. The development tab: about $1 billion.

The Prius caught on quicker in Japan than the company had expected. Toyota doubled production to 2,000 cars a month and sold nearly 18,000 in the first year. But the Prius did not receive the same warm reception when the first few right-hand-drive models arrived in the United States in May of 1999. A group of potential buyers in southern California found a lot to complain about (for example, the trunk was so small it wouldn't even hold a baby stroller), and American Toyota executives worried if there would be a market for the car. The complaints were heard in Japan. When left-hand-drive models finally arrived in the United States, the Prius had been upgraded with more power, cleaner emissions, and a lighter battery pack. Still, the executives and Toyota dealers worried—and while they did, rival Honda introduced its hybrid Insight to the American public in December of 1999.

The Prius, which is Latin for *first* or *before*, did not go on sale until July of 2000, and the early reviews were not kind. But the reviewers were not the customers. The Prius caught on anyway and sales were higher than anyone inside or outside the company had believed possible.

In the second half of 2000, a total of 5,562 cars was sold. In 2001, the first full calendar year, the total reached 13,388. The numbers have been on the rise ever since. With nearly 108,000 sales in 2005, the Toyota Prius was the runaway leader among hybrid vehicles in the United States. The gas-electric sedan

By the end of 2001, Toyota had sold nearly 19,000 Prius sedans to United States motorists.

eclipsed its closest rival, the Honda Civic Hybrid, by a four-to-one margin and accounted for more than half of all U.S. hybrid sales. By the end of April 2006, worldwide sales of the Prius reached 504,700. Along the way, the car has accumulated a number of prestigious awards. *Car and Driver* magazine, one of the early naysayers, gave its "One of the 10 Best" accolade to the Prius in 2004.

Toyota, with its upscale Lexus division, has emerged as the world leader in gas-electric hybrid technology and sales. In 2005, with two Toyota models and one Lexus hybrid vehicle, it sold 235,000 hybrid vehicles globally and more than 145,000 in the United States, accounting for about three-fourths of the U.S. hybrid market. Two additional models were introduced in the first half of 2006: the mainstream Toyota Camry Hybrid sedan and the expensive, performance-oriented Lexus GS 450h. In March of 2006, the company announced sales of all its hybrid models had passed the 600,000 mark.

Hybrid Sales: 1999–2005

Hybrid Model	1999	2000	2001	2002	2003	2004	2005
Honda Insight	17	3,788	5,789	2,216	1,168	583	666
Toyota Prius		5,562	13,388	20,119	24,627	53,991	107,897
Honda Civic				15,658	21,729	25,571	25,864
Chevrolet Silverado (FAS)						2,000	4,000 (est.)
GMC Sierra (FAS)						500	1,000 (est.)
Ford Escape						2,987	15,583
Honda Accord						1,636	16,826
Lexus RX 400h							21,263
Toyota Highlander							17,352
Mercury Mariner							283
Total	**17**	**9,350**	**19,177**	**37,993**	**47,524**	**87,268**	**210,737**

Source: J. D. Power and Associates, 2006, The McGraw-Hill Companies, Inc.

What the Owners Say: Toyota Prius

Arlene Sheff wasn't really looking for a new car. But the psychotherapist from Columbia, Maryland, was struck by one particular topic while attending a forum on women's issues: *What is our legacy to our grandchildren?* "That's when I decided that I must do something for the environment," she recalled. "That would be my contribution."

It was love at first test drive. "I thought the car was fun," she recalled. "Its size felt right and it has a lot of really good features . . . and I also like that it will get great gas mileage."

What about the price premium for a hybrid? "I didn't worry about the cost," she said. "My concern is about the environment." For the record, the Sheffs like Arlene's Prius so much that husband Bob bought one a few months later.

Another Maryland resident, Renee Lowden, decided to buy her Toyota Prius about two years after her husband, Michael, purchased his Honda Civic Hybrid. "My main reason is to reduce our dependence on oil. It's unconscionable the way we say we don't want to be dependent on oil and then we go ahead and use it without changing our habits." She loves everything about the car and said it has had a marked effect on her driving habits. "I'm the one going up the hill at three miles an hour and down the hill at ninety miles an hour," she joked.

A Good Try from the U.S.

Credit for development of the modern hybrid car belongs rightfully to Japanese manufacturers Toyota and Honda. But it didn't have to be that way.

The United States could have had a twenty-five year head start on the rest of the world if only someone in government or the U.S. automotive industry had paid serious attention to Dr. Victor Wouk.

Wouk and a partner, Dr. Charles L. Rosen, formed Petro-Electric Motors and developed the first full-size, full-power hybrid car in 1974. It was a modified 1972 Buick Skylark, powered by a Mazda rotary engine and an electric motor.

The electric motor was used for starting and for boosting power and its batteries were recharged during braking. However, a fully independent electrical source had not been developed within the automobile so the batteries also had to be charged by an external source of electricity.

Nevertheless, the car met the strictest emissions standards of the day, got 30 miles per gallon of gasoline, and had a top speed of 85 miles per hour.

Wouk, an electrical engineer, and Rosen, a chemical researcher, were motivated to build a hybrid car more by concerns about air pollution than fuel efficiency. The federal Clean Air Act of 1970 required that auto emissions be reduced by 95%.

The law led to the start of the Environmental Protection Agency's Clean Car Incentive Program, which was meant to spur innovative designs by the auto industry and inventors.

Wouk's hybrid car met the strict standards, but the EPA was unconvinced that hybrid power was viable and declined to continue its support. Wouk fought for two years to get the decision reversed before Petro-Electric ran out of money and he gave up the fight.

Still, Wouk remained a passionate advocate of hybrid power for the rest of his life. When Toyota brought the Prius to the United States, Wouk bought one, but admitted that the technology had advanced considerably from the system he developed for the Skylark. The brother of novelist Herman Wouk, Victor died in 2005.

Is a Hybrid Car for You?

Did You Hear the One About . . .

A young man purchased one of the original Volkswagen Beetles and soon started bragging to his associates about the car's great gasoline mileage. Week after week, he reported back. "I'm averaging 25 miles per gallon. Last week I got 27 miles per gallon." And on and on it went, until everyone tired of his talk.

So his fellow employees devised a plan. Each day one person snuck out to the Volkswagen and added a little fuel. Sure enough, the reports came back, more glowing with each telling: 28 mpg, 29, 33, 40. The little Volkswagen just kept getting better.

Then the employees switched tactics. Each day they removed a little fuel. The mileage went down— 37, 34, 32 mpg—and so did the bragging. Eventually, the broad grins turned to frowns and the reports mysteriously stopped.

Finally, a fellow worker could not stand the silence. "How's it going with your Beetle?" he asked. "Well," the owner replied, "I don't know what has happened. The mileage keeps slipping. Last tank, I only averaged 18 miles a gallon. I have to take it in to the shop."

Did the employees ever tell the VW bug owner what they were up to? Nobody's ever said,

Did this really happen? Who's to say?

There is a lot to think about when considering the purchase a new car or truck. The information in this section will help you to determine if a hybrid is the right choice.

Hybrids Are Better for the Environment

There is no magic in the way hybrid cars help the environment: they simply use less gasoline. When an internal engine burns gasoline, it produces poisonous by-products that are pushed into the atmosphere through the tailpipe. Less gasoline equals less polution.

There are four main pollutants: hydrocarbons, a major contributor to urban smog, which is also toxic; nitrogen oxides, another smog producer and a contributor to acid rain; carbon monoxide, a product of incomplete combustion that reduces the blood's ability to carry oxygen and is dangerous to people with heart disease; and carbon dioxide, which is considered to be a contributor to global warming.

Catalytic converters and other controls have been successful in reducing the amount of pollutants produced by the internal combustion engine for each mile traveled, but their value has been offset by the substantial increase in miles traveled each year. Therefore, the best remaining remedy is to reduce gasoline consumption.

For a good example of why hybrid cars shine, look at statistics supplied by the U.S. Department of Energy. According to the department, a Toyota Prius will emit an average 3.4 tons of greenhouse gases into the atmosphere annually—a far cry from the 6.6 tons a conventional Camry will spew from its tailpipe over the same distance.

Hybrids Are Here to Stay

If you're thinking about buying a hybrid car but worry you may be stuck with a white elephant as soon as the fad wears off, put your mind at ease. Yes, the market is small now. But it is growing, and the rate of growth may well climb as manufacturers come out with new and different hybrid vehicles. It will no doubt accelerate if gasoline prices continue their upward spiral.

Based on a 2006 survey conducted before the sudden spurt in gasoline prices, J. D. Power and Associates Automotive Forecasting Services predicted that sales of hybrid cars will balloon to more than 856,000 by 2013. It also forecasted that the number of hybrid models will grow from eleven to fifty-two. But, the analysts noted, that would still represent only 4.7% of the annual automotive market.

Sales Forecasts through 2013								
Total Sales	**2006**	**2007**	**2008**	**2009**	**2010**	**2011**	**2012**	**2013**
U.S. Sales	16,908,971	17,050,440	17,268,663	17,480,572	17,683,952	17,878,550	18,061,983	18,255,195
U.S Hybrid Sales	256,557	352,372	514,114	676,572	734,266	804,639	839,507	856,343
U.S. Market Share	1.5%	2.1%	3%	3.9%	4.2%	4.5%	4.6%	4.7%

Source: J. D. Power and Associates Forecasting Hybrid Vehicle Outlook 2006 Q1
The McGraw-Hill Companies Inc.

Mike Chung, industry analyst for Edmunds.com, a top Web site for learning about all things automotive, believes that hybrid vehicles may account for about 2% of the market in 2007. However, he said, "It's so hard to project beyond next year. So much is dependent on which manufacturers are going to be involved . . . But I don't see hybrids going away any time soon because they work just like regular cars."

The future size of the hybrid market may be uncertain, but it appears the future of the hybrid vehicle is not. There are about a dozen hybrid vehicles available now, and there are a lot more on the way. As a prospective hybrid buyer, you will see a growing variety of choices.

Will You Save Enough on Gas to Justify the Price?

If there has been one major sticking point among potential buyers, it has been price. Because of the cost of the technology, hybrid vehicles—which range in price from about $20,000 to more than $60,000—are priced thousands of dollars higher than their thirstier counterparts. *Consumer Reports* magazine studied the costs of hybrid ownership compared with similar all-gas models in early 2006 and concluded that after five years of ownership and 75,000 miles, only two models will enjoy any cost benefits. The owner of a Toyota Prius will save $400, the magazine estimated, and the owner of a Honda Civic Hybrid will save $300. However, four other hybrids studied by the magazine had price premiums ranging from $1,900 to $5,500 over the same period of time. The *Consumer Reports* analysis was completed in spring 2006 so the cost-benefit ratio for hybrid vehicles may have changed somewhat depending on the current price of gasoline.

Nevertheless, other factors are more important in bringing the cost of hybrids into line with their traditional counterparts. A surge in sales would stimulate competition and result in lower prices, a pattern that typically occurs when a new product is brought into the marketplace. Advances in technology and a streamlining of production costs will have the same effect. The engineers at Toyota believe the day will come, perhaps sooner rather than later, when gas-electric automobiles will be priced much closer to traditionally powered cars.

In another survey, the editors of *Popular Mechanics* magazine found some owners expressed dissatisfaction because their real-world fuel mileage did not match the figures predicted by the U.S. Environmental Protection Agency. However, when the editors compared similar hybrid and traditionally powered cars, they still found the hybrids were significantly easier on fuel. For example, a Honda Civic Hybrid averaged 39.6 mpg in city driving and 42.7 mpg on the highway. That compared with 33.6 mpg around town and 36.3 mpg on the open road for a regular Honda Civic.

If you are considering the purchase of a hybrid vehicle, keep in mind that *Consumer Reports* based its calculations on an average motorist driving 15,000 miles a year. Your decision should be based on your car usage and the price of gasoline. If you drive only a few thousand miles a year, a hybrid car may never make economic sense. But if you are a high-mileage driver—say a sales representative or long-distance commuter—you can save a significant amount of money, regardless of gas prices, and your savings may be evident long before five years.

Putt-Putt Pollution

If you are concerned about the amount of pollutants your automobile spills into the atmosphere, you might want to be thinking about your lawn mower, too.

According to studies, the average power mower will put out as many pollutants in one hour's work as a typical car emits in a 100-mile journey. Or, to put it another way, the California Air Resources Board says that, gallon for gallon, a 2006 lawn mower engine contributes ninety-three times more smog-forming emissions than 2006 cars.

The Environmental Protection Agency is considering regulations that would mandate catalytic converters for small gasoline engines.

Battlefield Hybrids

In times of war, the elements of speed and surprise almost invariably give a fighting force tactical advantage over its adversaries. But it's hard to sneak up on the enemy in big cargo trucks that are so noisy their occupants can't even talk to each other.

That's one reason why the U.S. Army and Marines are investigating hybrid power as they search for the next generation of vehicles that will transport the troops and their supplies. If these rugged vehicles can be made to run reliably on electric power alone, they could cover crucial ground in near-silence.

But silence isn't the only reason—and not even the primary one—why the military is testing hybrid power for vehicles that will one day replace the Humvees, Jeeps, light trucks, armored vehicles, and probably even emergency vehicles and garbage trucks.

The No. 1 priority is increasing fuel efficiency. With fighting vehicles, extended range could increase the chances of survival when troops are on the move. With all of the support vehicles, it could simply mean a huge savings.

There's one other very important attribute of a hybrid vehicle that could play a huge role on the battlefield, as well as during natural disasters: the vehicle can generate electricity. With its conventional engine powering an onboard generator, the rechargeable batteries could supply electricity where none is now available.

For the military, this could mean electricity for field command posts, or even battlefield medical facilities. In natural disasters, such as Hurricane Katrina, hybrid vehicles could temporarily restore power in critical locations after power lines have been severed.

Side-by-Side Comparisons: Hybrid vs. Gas-Powered

Fuel mileage estimates supplied by the U.S. Environmental Protection Agency may be useful for comparative purposes, but they seldom are an accurate reflection of what cars and light trucks actually achieve.

This can be frustrating to the owners of hybrid vehicles, because the EPA's antiseptic testing methods are particularly ill-suited to vehicles that have two different sources of power.

Fortunately, there is a more realistic way to determine the fuel saving benefits of a hybrid vehicle. The comparison should be made between the actual fuel consumption of a hybrid and the consumption of a comparable gasoline-powered vehicle.

In early 2006, staff members of *Road & Track* magazine took a road trip with a front-wheel-drive Ford Escape Hybrid sport-utility vehicle, a Honda Civic Hybrid sedan, and a Toyota Camry Hybrid sedan. Also along for the trip over roads of varying terrain and traffic conditions were the gasoline-engine counterparts of the trio.

At the end of their two-day trek around southern California they made their calculations. Here is what they came up with:

Mileage Comparison

	Average MPG	EPA estimates
Ford Escape Hybrid	29.9	36 city/31 highway
Ford Escape	19.9	22 city/26 highway
Honda Civic Hybrid	40.7	49 city/51 highway
Honda Civic	32.8	30 city/40 highway
Toyota Camry Hybrid	37.3	43 city/37 highway
Toyota Camry	26.3	21 city/29 highway

A few things become obvious from these figures: (1) With the surprising exception of the Toyota Camry, none of the vehicles was able to land squarely in the range of the government estimates. (2) The hybrid cars were significantly less thirsty than their gasoline counterparts. (3) The Honda Civic compact gasoline car required 11.5% more fuel than the much bigger and heavier mid-size Toyota Camry Hybrid.

A good place for a person considering the purchase of a new vehicle to investigate fuel-economy figures is on the Internet at www.fueleconomy.gov. The site provides the EPA estimates for all vehicles and also offers real-world figures supplied by owners.

Other Cost Incentives

While most potential buyers of hybrid cars focus on fuel-cost savings, there are several other important benefits a hybrid owner will enjoy. Government, at the federal and state levels, is offering incentives for buyers to get cleaner, more efficient vehicles, and even the insurance industry is getting into the act. Several cost considerations beyond savings on gasoline work in favor of the hybrid car owner.

Federal tax breaks. Starting in calendar year 2006, the federal government offers tax credits to those who buy a hybrid vehicle. They are based on a complicated formula that allows the full deduction only for a manufacturer's first 60,000 sales, after which the credit decreases until it expires after fifteen months. The chart on page 20 was prepared by the American Council for an Energy Efficient Economy (ACEEE). Most of the figures are government-certified. The rest, as noted, are ACEEE estimates. Only one hybrid vehicle, the Honda Insight with manual transmission, did not qualify because of not passing emissions testing.

The 2005 law replaces a tax deduction that had been on the books since 1999. The big advantage of the updated rule is that a tax credit can be deducted directly from a person's federal income tax bill. The previous law reduced only the amount of the person's taxable income. But there is another side to the 2005 act.

Analyst Mike Chung believes that hybrid vehicles that have not yet reached the marketplace may reap the biggest benefit from the gradually declining tax benefits. That's because cars that are popular now will be the first to pass the 60,000 mark. For example, Toyota sold more than 107,000 Prius models in 2005 and was on pace to exceed that in 2006. That means the popular Prius is likely to be the first to lose its tax deduction.

State tax breaks. Some states have already enacted additional tax breaks for hybrid vehicle buyers and others are considering them. In addition, states have enacted, or are considering, other benefits such as use of a high-occupancy lane by hybrid vehicles occupied only by the driver. You can find out where your state stands on hybrid vehicle benefits by going to the Web site www.hybrid-center.org. In the category Hybrid Incentives, the site tracks what is happening in all fifty states.

Private industry incentives. American companies are jumping on the hybrid bandwagon, offering cash and other incentives to employees who buy fuel-efficient vehicles. As of mid-2006, these firms had put programs into place:

Hyperion, of Santa Clara, California, offers $5,000 to employees who buy hybrid vehicles.

Bank of America initiated a pilot program to reimburse employees in three locations $3,000 when they purchase a hybrid vehicle. The program covers

Tax Credits: 2006 Hybrids

Make	Model	Class of Vehicle	Adjusted City MPG	Amount of Credit
Chevrolet/GMC	Silverado/Sierra two-wheel drive	Pickup	18	$250 (estimated)
Chevrolet/GMC	Silverado/Sierra four-wheel drive	Pickup	17	$650 (estimated)
Ford	Escape Hybrid two-wheel drive	SUV	36	$2,600
Ford	Escape Hybrid four-wheel drive	SUV	33	$1,950
Honda	Accord Hybrid (without updated control calibration)	Car	25	$650
	(with updated control calibration)			$1,300
Honda	Civic Hybrid	Car	49	$2,100
Honda	Insight	Car	57	$1,450
Lexus	GS 450h	Car	25	$1,550
Lexus	RX 400h two-wheel drive	SUV	33	$2,200
Lexus	RX 400h four-wheel drive	SUV	31	$2,200
Mercury	Mariner Hybrid	SUV	33	$1,950
Saturn	VUE Green Line	SUV	27	$1,300 (estimated)
Toyota	Camry Hybrid	Car	40	$2,600
Toyota	Highlander Hybrid two-wheel drive	SUV	33	$2,600
Toyota	Highlander Hybrid four-wheel drive	SUV	31	$2,600
Toyota	Prius	Car	60	$3,150

Source: American Council for an Energy Efficient Economy (June 2, 2006)

21,000 employees living within 90 miles of Los Angeles, Boston, and the home office in Charlotte, North Carolina. The company said it would evaluate the program in late 2006 to determine if it should be offered to all 202,000 employees.

Google, based in Mountain View, California, offers $5,000 cash to purchase and $2,500 to lease low-emission cars—not just hybrids—that get at least 45 miles per gallon.

Timberland, of Stratham, New Hampshire, offers $3,000 to hybrid vehicle buyers who have worked at least two years for the company.

STMicroelectronics, Dallas, Texas, boosts monthly auto allowances by $83.34 for employees whose vehicles are rated between 39.2 and 46.9 miles per gallon of gasoline. Employees whose vehicles average 47 mpg or more get an extra $166.67 a month.

Patagonia, of Ventura, California, gives $2,000 to workers who buy hybrid or alternative-fuel vehicles.

Topics Entertainment of Seattle, Washington, offers $2,000 to employees who buy hybrids. It also offers $1,000 to employees who downgrade engine size in a new vehicle and doubles that amount if the employees switch from a V-8 engine to a four-cylinder one.

Integrated Archive Systems, Palo Alto, California, gives employees who have been with the company a year or more $10,000 toward the purchase of a hybrid vehicle.

My Organic Market (MOMS), Rockville, Maryland, gives employees $1,000 on the purchase of a car that gets an average of 45 miles per gallon or more. They also get an additional $1,000 at the end of each of the two years following their purchase if they still work at the company and still drive the car. To qualify, employees must be at the company for at least two years and work at least 1,000 hours a year.

The American Jewish Committee offers bonus payments of $2,500 or $1,500 to employees nationwide depending on which car they buy. The program covers hybrid vehicles as well as some compact cars.

Unfortunately, the Internal Revenue Service is not as generous as these employers. It has advised them that the cash incentives are considered compensation and must be reported on the employees' year-end tax statements.

Insurance discounts. There is one more piece of good financial news. Statistics show that the driver of a hybrid vehicle is less likely to get into an accident compared to the driver of a conventional car. As a result, the insurance industry is starting to get into the act. In February of 2006, Travelers Insurance began offering 10% discounts to hybrid car owners. By mid-year, the discounted policy was being offered in thirty-eight states and Travelers said it planned to make the cheaper insurance available nationwide. But there are restrictions, which vary from state to state. Another company, Farmers Insurance Group, announced in late 2005 it would offer a 5% discount to owners of hybrid or alternative-fuel

---

Hollywood Hybrids

Hybrid vehicles are not only for driving. To some people they are a symbol, a way of telling others that they care. That, apparently, is why they have gained such an enthusiastic following among the rich and famous—particularly the Hollywood rich and famous.

Anyone who has watched or read about the Academy Awards the past couple of years has seen a major shift in status symbols. Many of the "glitterati" have shunned the stretch limousine, long an ostentatious symbol of success, and are arriving at the big event in the leaner and greener hybrids or alternative-fuel vehicles, which are provided by manufacturers.

As part of the annual "Red Carpet, Green Cars" campaign sponsored by the environmental organization Global Green USA, a number of Hollywood stars were delivered to the 2005 Academy Awards and related events in Toyota or Lexus hybrid vehicles. Among them were Frances McDormand, Joaquin Phoenix, George Clooney, and Jennifer Aniston.

Similarly, Ford Motor Co. donated its hybrids and at least one alternative-fuel vehicle to transport stars during the festivities. Cathy Schulman, executive producer of best-motion-picture winner Crash, was provided with a Mariner. The entourage of best-supporting-actor nominee Jake Gyllenhaal arrived in a Ford Excursion running on biodiesel fuel.

Many stars have been even more closely associated with hybrid vehicles. Among those who have been identified as owners are Leonardo DiCaprio, Cameron Diaz, Ed Begley Jr., Brad Pitt, Will Ferrell, Kirsten Dunst, Larry David, Ed Norton, Donny Osmond, Johnny Depp, and Ashton Kutcher.

When it comes to what they drive, a lot of Hollywood's hot shots are advocates of conspicuous non-consumption.

vehicles in California. It was not clear in mid-2006 if the discount will spread throughout the industry. If you own a hybrid vehicle, you should check with your insurance company to see if it offers one.

Surveys of hybrid car buyers have shown repeatedly that price is not the primary factor in their purchase decision. Felix Kramer, founder and lead spokesman for the California Cars Initiative, a group devoted to promoting fuel efficient, nonpolluting automotive technologies, believes the whole issue of cost needs to be put into perspective.

He pointed out that, "When a person orders a car with a sunroof, or a leather interior, or any other option, nobody asks, 'What's the payback?' Those options are simply for the convenience and enjoyment of the owner. The extra cost of a hybrid should be viewed the same way. It's the price of the environmental feature. Less frequent trips to the pump and cheaper fuel from electricity are icing on the cake."

The owner of a 2006 Honda Civic Hybrid, who listed himself on the Internet only as Nick of Indianapolis, feels the same way. "People never question drivers of cars with options about when they will pay for themselves. It is just a lifestyle choice."

For Rich Kreuger, a Michigan resident, the purchase of a Ford Escape Hybrid came only after an intense study of the technology and its benefits. He now finds it has brought him enjoyment he hadn't counted on and admission into a select group of dedicated motorists. "I am incredibly satisfied with it, and I intend to continue to buy hybrids," he'll tell anyone who asks.

Some of his reasons: "It's one hell of a conversation piece." "There's a sense of superiority knowing you have such an advanced and efficient vehicle working for you." "In some ways I find myself a pioneer and a respected person for getting the most out of my hybrid." "There's a sense of belonging that's very comforting."

He will tell you there are a couple of other things he likes about his Escape Hybrid, too. "To be different . . . [to have] an SUV that gets better miles per gallon than most cars. Nyah! Nyah! Oh yeah, and that green goodie goodie environmental stuff."

Do You Want to Make a Statement?

Has anyone ever called you a metrospiritual? Do you prefer organic wine with your dinner? Are you in a demographic category called Lifestyles of Health and Sustainability (LOHAS, according the the experts)? Are your purchases ruled more by your heartstrings than your pursestrings?

If so, you have been identified by the marketing mavens as part of a $227 billion sector of the population whose buying habits are strongly influenced by their personal values—and that puts you squarely in a group that makes you a prime candidate for the purchase of a hybrid car.

Beliefs and lifestyle aside, however, it turns out that hybrid buyers are surprisingly mainstream in their buying habits, if not in their choice of vehicles. Lonnie Miller, director of industry analysis for R. L. Polk & Co., said a recent analysis by his company "showed that the hybrid demographic is really not that different from the typical car buyer."

The bulk of all hybrid vehicle buyers (a full 74%) are between the ages of 35 and 64, Miller said. The rest are divided nearly equally in the under-35 and over-64 brackets. According to Miller, that's pretty much the age breakdown for all car buyers.

Miller also reported that hybrid vehicle buyers basically fit into the same income brackets as the purchasers of conventional cars. Approximately 35% have annual household incomes of $50,000 to $100,000, another 22% have incomes ranging from $100,000 to $150,000, and 24% earn more than $150,000. Only about 18% have incomes less than $50,000.

If money cannot buy you happiness, it can at least purchase some comfort. That's just as true of the hybrid vehicle buyer as it is of any other car purchaser. "Forty-seven percent of the people who bought the Lexus RX 400, [a hybrid luxury sport-utility vehicle] have incomes of more than $150,000 a year," the Polk analyst noted.

The marketers know where hybrid buyers live, too. The Polk data lists the top five states, in order, as California, Florida, Texas, New York, and Virginia. The top five cities, according to Polk, are Los Angeles, San Francisco, New York, Washington, D.C., and Boston.

Evaluate the Downside

You now know something about why people buy hybrid cars. People feel good by doing their part to save fuel and blunt the contribution of car exhaust to atmospheric pollution. But that doesn't necessarily make the purchase any easier. You may feel that the technology is still pretty much of a mystery; you may still have questions and concerns.

If so, you may find some answers in a recent poll. With the help of Harris Interactive, the Kelly Blue Book Web site (www.kbb.com) polled prospective hybrid car buyers and learned what was on their minds. Those concerns were investigated by a cable news network Web site, CNN.com, in March of 2006 and here is what the investigators found:

1. Hybrid cars have expensive technology that is difficult and expensive to fix. All of today's new cars are controlled by computers and complicated electronics that must be diagnosed and repaired with the use of expensive equipment generally found only in the service department of an authorized dealer. The

day of the do-it-yourself "shade tree mechanic" is over, with the exception of some routine maintenance and minor repairs. Hybrid-specific parts generally have long warranties that insulate owners from their replacement costs.
Conclusion: It's only a slight concern.

2. Hybrids have limited battery-pack life. To assure long battery life, hybrid cars are designed so that the batteries are never fully charged nor fully discharged. In addition, manufacturers guarantee the batteries for many years. Toyota's warranty is for eight years or 100,000 miles. Honda and Ford warranties cover eight years or 80,000 miles.
Conclusion: It's not a major concern.

3. Hybrid cars sometimes stall, stutter, and sputter. This worry has apparently arisen from a Toyota Prius software problem in 2005. Toyota recalled and fixed all of the vehicles that experienced shutoff while the cars were being driven, and all Priuses produced since contain the software that eliminates the problem.
Conclusion: It's not a real concern.

4. Hybrid cars will not return enough savings in reduced fuel usage to overcome their initial higher cost. *Consumer Reports* and others have found that it is hard to justify the purchase of a hybrid car simply as a money-saver. Fuel costs will be considerably less, but they won't offset the initial higher cost and greater depreciation. Even a federal tax write-off won't bring the cost of most hybrid cars into balance with comparable cars powered by traditional powerplants.
Conclusion: Depending on how much driving you do, this could be a legitimate concern.

5. Hybrid cars do not offer sufficient driving performance. All hybrid vehicles have enough power for safe acceleration, hill climbing, passing, and merging in today's traffic conditions. However, with a couple of exceptions, they are not road rockets.
Conclusion: You have to choose your priorities.

6. Hybrids do not hold their resale value. The CNN.com editors declared that with the exception of the unique Toyota Prius, this has generally been true. But resale value is always dependent on demand. Since mid-2006, when gas prices jumped to nearly $3 per gallon, used hybrids—the Insight, Civic, and Prius—appear to be holding their value well. Prospective buyers who may be concerned can research the sale- and purchase-price estimates at www.edmunds.com or www.kbb.com.

Conclusion: This may or may not be a genuine cause for concern. But keep one thing in mind: hybrids won't be that easy to resell unless another hybrid enthusiast comes along.

7. Hybrids don't get the fuel mileage promised. If you are calculating how much money you will save on fuel by looking at Environmental Protection Agency estimates, you will be disappointed. However, you will be disappointed with any car you buy because EPA numbers are determined with testing methods that do not hold up in the real driving world. That said, if real-world driving produces results that are 15% lower than EPA figures, a person who expects to get 50 mpg will probably be a lot more disappointed than the person who expects to get 25 mpg.

Conclusion: Assume your figures will be lower than the estimates. Whether that's a concern is up to you.

02:
{A Buyer's Guide to Hybrids}

There's a whole lot of complicated work going on beneath the surface of most hybrid vehicles. A gasoline engine and an electric motor work independently or in harmony to propel the vehicle *and* to generate electricity. A complicated transmission optimizes the efficiency of the powerplant. High-powered batteries supply the juice to the motor. Sophisticated electronics coordinate the action.

Yet, all that chugging, whirring, shifting, switching, and generating takes place unseen, unheard, and almost unfelt from inside the cabin. To the driver, a hybrid vehicle works almost exactly like one powered by a conventional internal combustion engine. It may not be magic, but it's close.

We'll be taking a detailed look at what's available, what it costs, and what it's like to drive a hybrid vehicle. But first, let's take a layman's look at this artful application of automotive engineering.

How Today's Hybrid Cars Work

The only practical form of hybrid power in the United States now mates a gasoline engine with one or more electric motors. The reason is simple: gasoline is the only universally available, government-approved automotive fuel in all fifty states.

New regulations to reduce the sulfur in diesel fuel may soon lead to the production of diesel-electric hybrids that can be sold in all fifty states—but none was on the horizon in the summer of 2006.

There are two primary advantages to hybrid powerplants: they are more fuel efficient than an internal combustion engine, and they release fewer pollutants into the atmosphere. But there are disadvantages, too. They cost significantly more to make and require a heavy, space-robbing battery pack to store the electricity.

As a result, different manufacturers have taken different approaches to the technology. That is why there are four types of hybrid power in use or under pre-production development for cars and light trucks sold in the United States.

It's easy for a Toyota Prius driver to know where the power is coming from.

The Four Types of Hybrid Powerplant

Full hybrid. The full hybrid powerplant is one that can run on just the gasoline engine, just an electric motor, or a combination of both. This is the most widely used system and powers hybrids of the Toyota and Ford motor companies. While the electric motor acts primarily as an assist to the gasoline engine, it also gets the vehicle moving from a stop and can propel the car by itself in certain situations. Because the electric motor is always on call, engineers can modify the gasoline engine to reduce power in favor of fuel efficiency. Gas mileage easily exceeds that of a comparably powered conventional vehicle in most driving sit-

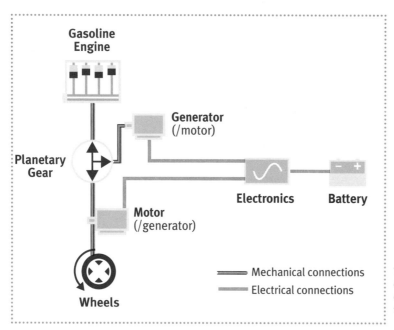

The full hybrid vehicle can be powered by either its gasoline engine or electric motor, or with both power sources working together.

uations, but the hybrid setup does its best fuel-saving work in city driving for two reasons: the engine shuts off when the car is stopped in traffic, and the car can be propelled by the electric motor alone under certain conditions.

Assist hybrid. Like the full hybrid, the assist hybrid powerplant uses an electric motor to boost the power of its internal combustion engine, and it has an auto off/on feature when the vehicle stops in traffic. Where it differs is that the electric motor does not usually power the car by itself, so the gasoline engine runs whenever the car is moving. Exceptional fuel mileage is the direct result of a small, efficient gasoline engine getting a boost from the electric motor. Honda's Integrated Motor Assist is an example of this system, with one exception. In its newest 2006 Civic Hybrid, the manufacturer has managed to engineer its powertrain in a way that the electric motor can power the vehicle by itself during infrequent situations involving low speeds and a light load.

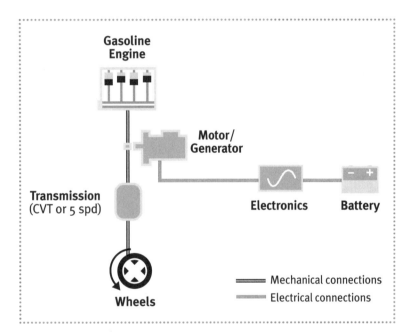

In the assist-hybrid vehicle, the electric motor acts primarily to give the gasoline engine more power when needed.

Mild hybrid. The fuel-saving system employed on several current General Motors pickup trucks is called a mild hybrid, although it does not technically fulfill the requirements of a hybrid because its electric motor does not help propel the vehicle. Instead, the motor-generator replaces the vehicle's starter and alternator, allowing the engine to shut down and automatically restart at traffic stops without disruption to auxiliary systems such as air-conditioning. The electric motor can also reverse itself to generate electricity that replenishes the 42-volt battery.

Two-mode hybrid. The two-mode hybrid system—a joint project of General Motors, DaimlerChrysler, and BMW that will reach production in 2007—employs two electric motors fully integrated with four fixed mechanical gear ratios inside the vehicle's electronically variable transmission. Sophisticated electronics direct the system to select the most efficient operation point for the power level demanded by the driver. Developers say the system can increase composite (city and highway) fuel economy by 25%.

The first mode provides fuel-saving capability in low-speed, stop-and-go driving. It can operate three ways: with power provided by the engine alone, and power provided by the electric motor alone, power provided by a combination of electric propulsion and engine power.

The second mode is used primarily at high speeds to optimize fuel economy while providing full engine power when conditions demand it, such as trailer towing or climbing steep grades.

The consortium says there are several advantages to the setup. It saves fuel in both city and highway driving. Its overall size and mechanical content are similar to a conventional automatic transmission. It can operate in infinitely variable ratios or the four fixed gear ratios. It can be tailored for use with existing automotive engines, regardless of size or type, and can be applied to vehicles with rear-wheel drive, front-wheel drive, or all-wheel drive.

Its developers say it will be particularly useful in vehicles that require large engines for carrying heavy loads, towing, or hill climbing. The battery pack is larger than a typical automotive battery, but it is being designed to fit in a vehicle without compromising passenger space. The two-mode hybrid system will first appear in Chevrolet Tahoe and GMC Yukon full-size sport-utility vehicles in late 2007.

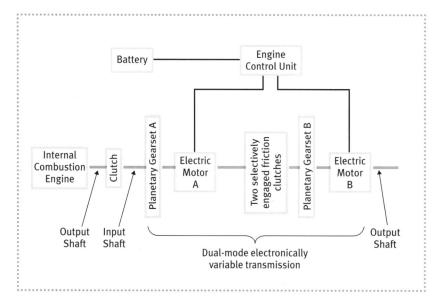

In the two-mode hybrid, the electric motors boost a vehicle's power from within the transmission.

A Buyer's Guide to Hybrids

Driving Forces in the Hybrid Powerplant

All by itself, the hybrid powerplant is something of a modern engineering marvel. But, the engineers didn't call it quits there. They pulled a few other technological tricks out of their toolboxes to further improve fuel efficiency and add luster to its clean-and-green image. Here's what they came up with.

Regenerative braking: powering the battery. Scientists have been trying since the dawn of the automotive age to develop an electrical storage system small enough and powerful enough to run an automobile on electricity alone. The technology has improved over the years, and there are indications of further breakthroughs to come, but the battery has not yet been devised that can provide enough sustained power to make an electric car useful. Under ideal conditions, a

Regenerative braking occurs when a hybrid vehicle is coasting or being stopped. The electric motor that supplements the vehicle's power reverses itself to become a generator. When that happens, the generator helps slow the vehicle down while producing electricity to charge the battery.

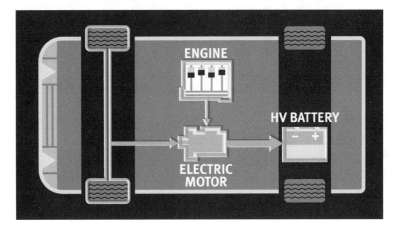

battery-powered car has a range of less than a hundred miles and cannot be recharged quickly—deeming it hopelessly inefficient for long-distance travel.

As a result, the only way to make an electric motor practical for automotive use is to keep the battery pack charged while the car is in motion. In hybrid cars, this is accomplished in part by a bit of scientific wizardry known as *regenerative braking*.

Whenever a driver takes his foot off the gas pedal, the same electric motor that helps to power the wheels reverses itself, becomes a generator, and supplies electricity to the battery pack while helping to slow the car down. In most circumstances, if the driver puts his foot on the brake to slow the car more quickly, the generation of electricity is accelerated.

Of course, when needed, the gasoline engine operates the generator to produce electricity for the batteries, too.

Saving fuel by shutting down. Here, another bit of unconventional technology is at work in all hybrid vehicles. When they are brought to a full stop, say at a red traffic signal, the gasoline engine shuts down, saving fuel and temporarily eliminating all noxious exhaust gases.

When the light turns green, the driver simply moves his foot from the brake to the accelerator and the electric motor starts the engine. There is no need for a starter motor. There is an almost undetectable hiccup when the gasoline engine re-fires, but it soon becomes an unnoticed part of the hybrid driving experience.

The gasoline engine automatically shuts off when a hybrid vehicle is brought to a stop at a traffic signal. This saves fuel and reduces exhaust emissions. When the driver moves his foot from the brake to the accelerator, the electric motor turns the engine back on almost seamlessly.

Continuously variable transmission. A third feature on the vast majority of current hybrid vehicles is the continuously variable transmission. It does not have the traditional fixed set of forward gears. Instead, it is able to continuously adjust gear ratios to optimize efficient power use among the electric motors and the gasoline engine. While it is smoother than a conventional transmission, its operation might seem unusual—even unpleasant, at first. When a driver steps on the accelerator, the engine speeds up immediately and the transmission jockeys the gear ratios seamlessly as it selects the best way to transmit the power to the wheels. The feel is akin to a slipping clutch on a manual transmission car. The sound, although much quieter, has been described as similar to a propeller plane taking off or a powerboat accelerating.

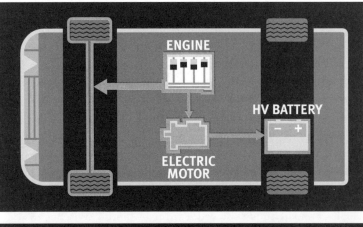

The hybrid vehicle's gasoline engine serves two purposes. It puts power to the wheels and, when needed, it helps the electric motor/generator recharge the battery.

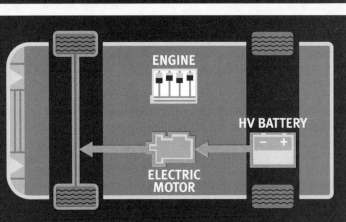

In a full-hybrid vehicle, the electric motor alone can supply all the power under certain conditions.

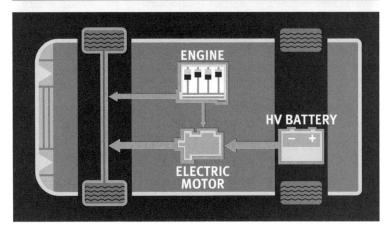

When a burst of power is needed, the gasoline engine and electric motor work together to provide maximum thrust.

Defusing Electrical Worries

It takes a lot of electricity to operate the powerful electric motors, air-conditioning, heater, lights, power steering, and assorted other functions in a gasoline-electric hybrid vehicle. That's why they have battery packs ranging from 300 to 650 volts and that's why buyers and accident responders have voiced concerns. A 60-volt jolt could be enough to kill you.

But there really is little cause for worry. During the years hybrids have been on the road (2000 through June 2006), there were no documented deaths caused by electrical shocks, according to the National Highway Safety Administration.

Wade Hoyt, a spokesman for Toyota, which has sold more than 600,000 hybrid vehicles, went a step further. "We have no reports of injuries related to the hybrid battery or electrical systems from any of our hybrid vehicles," he said.

The simplest precaution anyone can take is to simply turn off the ignition and remove the key. That turns off the power just the same as throwing the master switch to disengage electricity in a home.

But getting to the key may not possible if a hybrid car is in a serious accident. That's why the manufacturers have built in additional safety systems. In Toyotas, the power is shut off as soon as an airbag is deployed. Ford uses inertia switches to disable its system in a crash.

Honda has two different procedures for cutting power if the ignition key cannot be reached. Remove the main fuse from the fuse box located under the hood on the driver's side of the engine compartment; or cut both cables to the 12-volt battery located under the hood. That cuts power to the high-voltage battery controllers and prevents electricity from flowing into the high-voltage cables.

In addition, high-voltage batteries are installed in sealed metal cases. Ford, Honda, and Toyota locate them behind the rear axle in a spot least likely to be damaged in a collision. Further, all three manufacturers make their high-voltage lines easy to spot by coloring their casings a bright orange.

Beyond that, the manufacturers offer online manuals that outline safety procedures, and their representatives conduct safety courses for emergency workers.

The bottom line, according to Jesus Almeida, a Honda safety instructor, is that hybrid vehicles pose no greater danger than any others if motorists and rescue personnel follow the proper procedures.

When you open the hood, the Hybrid Synergy Drive badge announces that there is a lot more than just a gasoline engine at work beneath the surface of a Toyota Camry Hybrid.

The world leader in the manufacture of hybrid vehicles, Toyota has five models in production: three by the Toyota division and two more by its premium Lexus division. All employ the full hybrid system that Toyota calls "Hybrid Synergy Drive." The Prius and Camry are front-wheel-drive sedans; the Toyota Highlander and Lexus RX 400h are front- or all-wheel-drive sport-utility vehicles, and the Lexus GS 450h is a rear-wheel-drive luxury/sports sedan. In April of 2007, Lexus will begin selling the Lexus LS 600h, a hybrid version of its very expensive, rear-wheel-drive flagship. It will be the first hybrid vehicle with a V-8 gasoline engine.

Dave Hermance, Toyota's executive engineer for advanced automotive technologies, confirmed that additional hybrid vehicles are under development, but he declined in June 2006 to say what they are. The Toyota brand, he said, will focus on hybrid vehicles that are fuel-economy oriented, while the Lexus division will build hybrids that are performance oriented.

While the basic hybrid technology has not changed since the first Prius was built, it is under constant refinement. "We are continuing to introduce new components each time we come out with a new hybrid car," he explained. As an example, he cited the latest hybrid, the Toyota Camry, which uses a fourth-generation battery, third-generation power electronics, a third-generation transmission, and a second generation of electric motors.

Toyota's hybrid vehicles, from left, are the Highlander, Camry, and Prius.

Regarding early concerns about battery life and high replacement costs, he said Toyota has run tests over 150,000 miles and has found no battery deterioration to that point. Although Toyota guarantees them for eight years or 100,000 miles, the company believes the batteries will last the life of the car.

As well as it already works, the modern hybrid car is still a work in progress. In addition to reducing costs, Hermance said, Toyota engineers are confident that improvements in future generations of hybrids will also make them run cleaner and more efficiently.

Clockwise from top left: Beyond that rear liftgate the Toyota Prius has lots of space for luggage. The Toyota Highlander Hybrid announces its presence to all it approaches. The instrument panel of the Toyota Highlander tells its drivers all they need to know.

Toyota Prius

Now in its second generation, the Toyota Prius was the first hybrid automobile to reach U.S. shores that could seat four people and meet the requirements of a small family. When it went on sale in July of 2000, it was hailed more for its fuel-efficient technology than its drivability. Still, testers at *Motor Trend* magazine were duly impressed after a cross-country journey from California to southern Florida. During that trip they found the front-wheel-drive sedan to be quite livable and surprisingly efficient. The *Motor Trend* team averaged 61.8 miles per gallon in city driving and 38.4 miles per gallon on the open road.

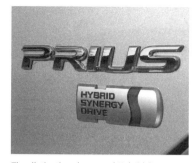

The distinctive shape and Hybrid Synergy Drive logo tell everyone a Toyota Prius owner cares about the environment.

The second-generation Prius, now being sold in Toyota dealerships, arrived in 2004. Bigger, roomier, and more aerodynamic than its predecessor, this hatchback sedan was the first to employ Hybrid Synergy Drive. The 1.5-liter engine, basically the same one used in the Toyota Echo, has been modified to run on the Atkinson cycle, which reduces power but increases efficiency. The power loss is offset, when needed, by a boost from the electric motor. The 0–60 mph time has improved from 13 seconds to 11, and fuel efficiency has climbed from an EPA-rated 52 miles per gallon in the city and 45 on the highway to 60 city/51 highway. A sampling of real-world users, however, indicates average fuel consumption has risen from about 45 to about 48 mpg.

Although the Prius has built an excellent reputation for low maintenance and superb dependability, the company in May 2006 announced a recall of 300,000 sedans (170,000 of them in the United States) to repair a potentially weak part of the steering-shaft assembly that could loosen or crack. The recall did not involve any of the hybrid powerplant components, and Toyota said no U.S. owners had complained about the steering.

In July, the company also announced a voluntary campaign to replace the crankshaft position sensor on certain 2001 through early 2002 Prius and Echo vehicles. Again, the recall did not involve any hybrid components.

With room for up to five passengers and 16 cubic feet of cargo space behind the foldable rear seatback, the Prius is now classified as a mid-size car. It comes

In 2005, Toyota sold 107,000 of these second-generation Prius sedans in the United States. The manufacturer expects to easily exceed that number in 2006.

with a generous amount of standard equipment, including an automatic climate control system that continues to operate when the engine is temporarily off. In the first-generation Prius, the air conditioner would stop working when the engine stopped.

A discreet rear spoiler makes the Toyota Prius more aerodynamic while its taillights and headlights complement the car's modern design.

Nick's Notes: The Prius is not exciting to drive, but it offers a comfortable ride, handles predictably, is easy to maneuver, and has sufficient power. It works well as a commuter car or a mommobile and returns its best fuel mileage in stop-and-go driving. This is because the engine shuts off completely each time the car is stopped and is then propelled by the electric motor alone from start-up until the gasoline engine's power is needed at approximately 15 miles per hour. But the car is also a relaxed, economical highway cruiser—capable of taking a family on its vacation or taking dad on a business trip.

The interior is not flashy, but materials are of high quality. The futuristic exterior sets the Prius apart from conventional cars, a desirable feature for conservationists and environmentalists who want the rest of the world to know they are practicing what they preach.

A week of mostly around-town driving in cold, damp weather, much of it in the rush-hour clog, proved to me that the Prius is a thoroughly practical and easy-to-use form of transportation. While its acceleration won't raise the hair on your neck, there is plenty of pep for jockeying in and out of traffic, passing, and entering freeways.

Toyota Prius Specifications

Type: front-wheel drive, four- or five-passenger hatchback

Base price: $21,725

Engine: 1.5-liter, 76-horsepower four-cylinder

Electric motor: 44 horsepower

Combined horsepower: 110

Battery: nickel-metal hydride

EPA fuel mileage: 60 mpg city / 51 highway

0–60 mph: 10.5 seconds

Emissions rating: Partial Zero–Ultra Low Emissions Vehicle

Transmission: continuously variable automatic

Brakes: anti-lock front disc/rear drum with brake assist and brake-force distribution

Steering: electrically powered rack-and-pinion

Suspension: independent with stabilizer bar in front; torsion beam and stabilizer bar at rear

Cargo space: 16.1 cubic feet

Curb weight: 2,986 pounds

Warranty: hybrid components—eight years, 100,000 miles; drivetrain—six years, 60,000 miles; bumper to bumper—three years, 36,000 miles

Standard safety features

seatbelts

driver and front passenger, front airbags

child-seat anchors

child safety locks

traction control

crumple zones and side-impact beams

Optional safety features

driver and front passenger, side airbags

front and rear side curtain airbags

stability control

tire pressure monitor

Major standard equipment

automatic climate control

cruise control

six-speaker stereophonic sound system with CD player

tilt-steering wheel with audio and climate controls

trip computer

push-button start

remote keyless entry

split 60/40 rear seatback

power windows, locks, and remote mirrors

Major optional equipment

backup camera

smart key system that allows owner to lock and unlock doors and start car without taking a key out of pocket or purse

upgraded, nine-speaker audio system with in-dash, six-CD player

Bluetooth capability for MP3 player, hands-free phone use

navigation system

high-intensity-discharge headlights with fog lights

leather seats and leather steering wheel

Two adults of almost any size fit comfortably in the front of a Toyota Prius.

Toyota Highlander Hybrid

The Toyota Highlander sport-utility vehicle can be purchased with front-wheel drive or all-wheel drive and in two trim levels: standard and limited. Toyota cautions that while all-wheel drive is the motorist's foul-weather friend, the Highlander has not been designed for off-road use. The ground clearance of the two-wheel-drive Highlander is only 6.9 inches and the all-wheel-drive version is elevated only 7.3 inches. From the outside, the Highlander Hybrid is pretty much identical to its thirstier, V-6-powered fraternal twin. Even the badging that announces the difference is anything but ostentatious.

The understated Toyota Highlander Hybrid can easily be mistaken for its gas-guzzling sibling.

Nick's Notes: Except for its steep initial price premium, the Toyota Highlander Hybrid is an excellent alternative to the conventional Highlander. It is peppier, more frugal, equally easy to drive, and just as versatile. Because of the extra battery weight, it doesn't handle quite as well—but that's hardly an issue when you are talking about a sport-utility vehicle. The interior of the vehicle is a bit bland, but it is well tailored and comfortable for front- and second-row passengers. Entry into the somewhat-pinched third-row seating is a bit difficult for adults, so it's best just to stow the children back there. Still, the Highlander is the only hybrid vehicle that even offers seven-passenger seating. The cargo area is easily accessed from the rear lift-gate, and there's enough space for a load of groceries when third-row seats are in place. With third and second rows folded flat, cargo space is cavernous.

The Highlander won't deliver the Environmental Protection Agency's fuel mileage estimates in most cases, but I averaged about 25 mpg of gasoline during a week of driving; over one two-day stretch, I got nearly 30 miles to the gallon.

You won't approach those numbers in any SUV of comparable size running on gasoline power alone. Unfortunately, for buyers who would measure the Highlander Hybrid against the conventional model strictly on a cost basis, it will not be easy to overcome the 30% higher price—even with a tax break.

Information and controls are easily accessible on the Toyota Highlander Hybrid center console.

The Toyota Highlander Hybrid offers only a modest reminder of its technological charms.

Lift that tailgate and the Toyota Highlander Hybrid can accept up to 80.6 cubic feet of cargo.

Toyota Highlander Hybrid Specifications

Type: front- or all-wheel drive, seven-passenger sport-utility vehicle

Base price: $33,030 (Standard), $39,296 (Limited)

Engine: 3.3-liter, 208-horsepower V-6

Front electric motor(s): 165 horsepower

Rear electric motor (AWD models): 67 horsepower

Combined horsepower: 268

Battery: nickel-metal hydride

EPA fuel mileage: 33 mpg city / 28 highway (2WD); 31/27 (AWD)

0–60 mph: 7.2 seconds (2WD), 7.8 seconds (AWD)

Emissions rating: Super Ultra Low Emissions Vehicle

Transmission: continuously variable automatic

Brakes: four-wheel, anti-lock disc brakes with brake assist and brake force distribution

Steering: electrically powered rack-and-pinion

Suspension: independent at all four wheels

Cargo space: 10.5 to 80.6 cubic feet

Curb weight: 4,070 (2WD), 4,244 pounds (AWD)

Warranty: hybrid-specific components—eight years, 80,000 miles; drivetrain—five years, 60,000 miles; bumper to bumper—three years, 36,000 miles

Standard safety equipment
   driver and front passenger, front and side
      airbags
   second-row side curtain airbags
   stability control
   traction control
   seatbelts
   side-impact door beams
   child-seat anchors
   child safety locks

Major standard features: Highlander Hybrid Standard
   air-conditioning
   six-speaker stereophonic sound system
   cruise control
   trip computer
   roof rack
   fold-flat second- and third-row seats
   power doors, locks, and mirrors
   eight-way adjustable power driver's seat

Major options: Highlander Hybrid Standard
   power sunroof
   eight-speaker premium sound system
   steering wheel with audio controls
   fog lights

Major standard features: Highlander Hybrid Limited
   climate control
   leather seats and wood-grain trim
   eight-speaker sound system with in-dash,
      six-CD player
   power sunroof
   trip computer
   roof rack
   fold-flat second- and third-row seats
   power doors, locks, and mirrors

Major options: Highlander Hybrid Limited
   navigation system

Clockwise from top left: The view is excellent from the high front seat of a Toyota Highlander Hybrid. The gauge on the left side of the instrument panel tells how much electricity the Toyota Highlander Hybrid is consuming. The Toyota Highlander Hybrid is a comfortable and economical choice for that family vacation. Behind the Toyota Highlander Hybrid's alloy wheels are strong anti-lock disc brakes.

Toyota Camry Hybrid

The Toyota Camry has been the best-selling mid-size sedan in the United States for nine of the last ten years, so the Japanese manufacturer has high hopes that the hybrid version will draw more mainstream buyers to its cleaner, more fuel-efficient powerplant. In fact, it has set its sights on 50,000 annual sales.

The 2.4-liter, four-cylinder gasoline engine is similar to the entry-level powerplant in the standard Camry, but like the Prius engine, it has been modified to operate on the fuel-saving Atkinson cycle. The resulting decrease in power is offset by the electric motor, which steps in to boost horsepower to 187, approximately the same as the V-6 engine in the last-generation Camry. The pay-off is shown by its EPA rating of 40 miles per gallon in the city, 38 on the highway, and an AT–PZEV (Advanced Technology–Partial Zero Emissions Vehicle) a rating that means it is 90% cleaner than the average new car.

Toyota hopes the all-new 2007 Camry will attract more buyers to hybrid power.

Nick's Notes: I had the opportunity to spend some limited driving time in a pre-production model and found it to be smooth, comfortable, and powerful enough to fill the requirements of a family car. Motorists looking for a corner-carving sports sedan need not apply, but everyone else should find its handling to be competent. The engine shut off imperceptibly at stoplights and started back up without hesitation as I pulled away. I suspect those EPA fuel-mileage figures will be hard to match in real-world driving conditions, but I did average 37 mpg driving in heavy traffic around New York City and in light traffic on the four-lane highways of northern New Jersey.

The 2007 Camry's styling is much more appealing than the forgettable look of its predecessor. But there is one downside to the Camry Hybrid. Because of the bulky battery pack, trunk space is reduced from 15 to 10.6 cubic feet. Based on Toyota's proven reliability and the lack of problems with all of its previous hybrid models, the newest hybrid should offer a satisfying ownership experience.

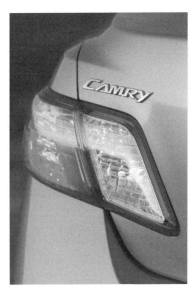

The 2007 Camry has a sleeker, more aerodynamic shape than its predecessors.

The Camry Hybrid instrumentation offers the driver a wealth of information about power usage.

Bold taillights make it clear to following cars that there's a Camry ahead.

Toyota Camry Hybrid Specifications

Type: front-wheel drive, five-passenger sedan
Base price: $25,900
Engine: 2.4-liter, 147-horsepower four-cylinder
Electric motor(s): 45 horsepower
Combined horsepower: 187
Battery: nickel-metal hydride
EPA fuel mileage: 40 mpg city / 38 highway
0–60 mph: 8.9 seconds
Emissions rating: Advanced Technology–Partial Zero Emissions Vehicle
Transmission: continuously variable automatic
Brakes: four-wheel, anti-lock disc brakes with brake assist and brake force distribution
Steering: electrically powered rack-and-pinion
Suspension: independent at all four wheels
Cargo space: 10.6 cubic feet
Curb weight: 3,680 pounds
Warranty: hybrid-specific components—eight years, 100,000 miles; drivetrain—six years, 70,000 miles; bumper to bumper—four years, 48,000 miles

Standard safety equipment
  driver and front passenger, front and side airbags
  front and rear side curtain airbags
  seatbelts
  driver's knee airbag
  tire pressure monitor
  stability control
  traction control
  side-impact door beams
  child-seat anchors
  child safety locks

Major standard features
  automatic on/off halogen headlights
  eight-speaker stereophonic sound system
  MP3/WMA recorder capability
  Bluetooth wireless technology
  cruise control
  trip computer
  dual-zone climate control
  power doors, locks, and mirrors
  power driver's seat
  smart key system with push-button start

Major options
  power sunroof
  premium sound system
  voice-activated navigation system
  leather seat trim
  heated front seats

The Camry's front bucket seats are comfortable and supportive.

A glance at the instrument panel will give a Camry Hybrid driver an instant readout of fuel consumption.

The new Camry is distinctive from any angle.

Lexus RX 400h

The Lexus RX 400h sport-utility vehicle is the country-club cousin of Toyota's community-pool Highlander. The two vehicles share many parts, but the Lexus has a built-in refinement that elevates it into a class that values pedigree as much as competence. Engines, transmission, brakes, steering, and suspension are identical, so the driving experience—and fuel efficiency—are essentially the same. And, like the Highlander, the all-wheel-drive Lexus is suited for slippery surfaces, but not off-roading because of its limited ground clearance. On the outside, the Lexus RX 400h is distinctively different from its cousin. It has stronger character lines that will not be confused with any other vehicle.

The sleek Lexus RX 400h is an upscale version of the mechanically identical Toyota Highlander Hybrid sport-utility vehicle.

Nick's Notes: From the captain's chair, this Lexus is pleasant, peppy, and easily controlled—just like the Highlander. To the passengers, however, the two vehicles are worlds apart. Lexus patrons are coddled and cosseted in a plush world of brushed aluminum, soft plastics, and polished veneer. Climate control and an upscale sound system are standard. Supple leather seats are listed as an option, but I have never seen a Lexus SUV that didn't have them. Other luxury-vehicle options include a rear-seat entertainment system and adaptive headlights, which help the driver see around corners. Front-seat passengers are wrapped in comfortable, supportive buckets with power adjustments. Second-row passengers have seats that can be moved back and forth, and seat-backs that recline.

Apparently figuring that such an upscale SUV was more the province of well-to-do empty nesters than a young family, Lexus chose to forego third-row seating in favor of that movable second-row bench. This not only makes the back seat a more comfortable environment for two or three adults, it increases minimum cargo space from 10.7 to 38.3 cubic feet. It's a much better arrangement for a golfing foursome headed to the country club.

Any way and anywhere you look at it, the Lexus RX 400h will not be mistaken for any other vehicle.

Lexus RX 400h Specifications

Type: front- or all-wheel drive, five-passenger sport-utility vehicle.

Base price: $45,355 (FWD), $46,755 (AWD)

Engine: 3.3-liter, 208-horsepower V-6

Front electric motor(s): 165 horsepower

Rear electric motor: 67 horsepower

Combined horsepower: 268

Battery: nickel-metal hydride

EPA fuel mileage: 31 mpg city / 27 highway

0–60 mph: 7.3 seconds (2WD), 7.9 seconds (AWD)

Emissions rating: Super Ultra Low Emissions Vehicle

Transmission: continuously variable automatic

Brakes: four-wheel, anti-lock disc brakes with brake assist and brake force distribution

Steering: electric powered rack-and-pinion

Suspension: independent at all four wheels

Cargo space: 38.3 to 84.7 cubic feet

Curb weight: 4,190 pounds (2WD), 4,365 pounds (AWD)

Warranty: hybrid-specific components—eight years, 100,000 miles; drivetrain—six years, 70,000 miles; bumper to bumper—four years, 48,000 miles

Standard safety equipment

driver and front passenger, front and
   side airbags
first- and second-row side curtain airbags
stability control
traction control
seatbelts
side-impact door beams
child-seat anchors
child safety locks

Major standard features

automatic on/off headlights
eight-speaker stereophonic sound system
cruise control
trip computer
roof rack
automatic climate control
power doors, locks, and mirrors
power rear liftgate
ten-way adjustable power driver's seat
eight-way adjustable front-passenger's seat
sliding, reclining rear seat
power sunroof

Major options

rear-seat entertainment system
voice-activated navigation system with
   backup camera
Mark Levinson audio system
leather seat trim
wood interior accents (with ivory leather interior)
adaptive, high-intensity-discharge headlights
heated front seats
headlight washers

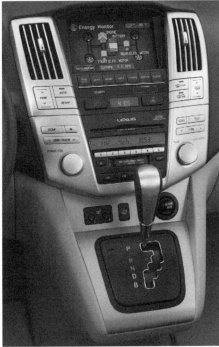

Whether it's in the mountains or among the swaying palms, the Lexus RX 400h instrumentation reports on the hybrid operation through the center console, left, and lets the driver know when he might be getting into trouble with the police, above.

Lexus GS 450h

The GS 450h represents a whole new direction for Toyota's hybrid technology. The powertrain was engineered more for performance than fuel efficiency, and it has been adapted to a rear-wheel-drive platform for the first time.

Consider this: the two-ton sedan can blister the macadam from a dead stop to 60 mph in 5.2 seconds—enough to put it in a dead heat with a Porsche 911 equipped with an automatic transmission. It also can keep pace with or outgun its V-8-powered rivals in the mid-size sports-luxury sedan segment all the way up to its governor-limited, 131-mph top speed.

But the fundamental mission of hybrid power has not been totally ignored, either. The GS 450h carves a cleaner path through the air than its conventional counterparts and, driven sensibly, it can return an EPA-rated 25 mpg of premium fuel in the city and 28 on the highway.

The principles that governed the engineering of the expensive GS 450h are not much different from those that underpin the entry-level Toyota Prius, but the execution required groundbreaking technology.

Hybrid Synergy Drive can be applied to rear-wheel-drive performance sedans as well as front-wheel-drive economy cars.

The solid handling of the Lexus GS 450h is most appreciated when the road turns twisty.

For this car, the engineers have combined a 3.5-liter V-6 engine, massaged to 292 horsepower, with a couple of powerful electric motors and a battery pack. Together they generate power equal to that of a 339-horsepower V-8.

The most challenging goal was development of a continuously variable transmission that could effectively deliver hybrid power to the rear wheels and take up approximately the same space as a conventional six-speed automatic transmission. It contains a two-stage torque multiplication device that essentially gives the electric motors a taller gear for speeds over 60 miles per hour. Other technical innovations include an advanced stability control system that goes to work when it anticipates driver loss of control, instead of after detecting it; electronically controlled brakes; and an optional suspension system that adjusts the front and rear sway bars to eliminate excessive body roll in turns. With a base price of $54,900, it replaces the V-8-powered GS 430 as the most expensive model among Lexus mid-size automobiles. It's earned its moniker as a "muscle hybrid."

Lexus GS 450h Specifications

Type: five-passenger, rear-wheel-drive sedan
Base price: $54,900
Engine: 3.5-liter, 292-horsepower V-6
Electric motor(s): 180 horsepower, 197 horsepower
Combined horsepower: 339
Battery: nickel-metal hydride
EPA fuel mileage: 25 mpg city / 28 highway
0–60 mph: 5.2 seconds
Emissions rating: Super Ultra Low Emissions Vehicle
Transmission: continuously variable automatic
Brakes: electronic four-wheel, anti-lock disc brakes with brake assist and brake force distribution
Steering: electric powered rack-and-pinion
Suspension: independent at all four wheels
Cargo space: 12.7 cubic feet
Curb weight: 4,134 pounds
Warranty: hybrid-specific components—eight years, 100,000 miles; drivetrain—six years, 70,000 miles; bumper to bumper—four years, 50,000 miles

Standard safety equipment

driver and front passenger, front and
    side airbags
overhead curtain airbags, first and second row
rear-passenger side airbags
driver and front passenger, knee airbags
stability control
traction control
seatbelts
rear back-up camera
side-impact door beams
child-seat anchors
child safety locks
tire pressure monitor

Major standard features

adaptive, automatic on/off headlights
ten-speaker stereophonic sound system
cruise control
automatic climate control
power doors, locks, and mirrors
parking assist system
heated and ventilated, power-operated driver's
    and front passenger's seats
remote keyless entry with push-button ignition
power sunroof
power rear sunshade
Bluetooth technology
leather seats and wood trim

Major options

voice-activated navigation system
fourteen-speaker Mark Levinson audio system
adaptive, high-intensity-discharge headlights
adaptive cruise control
pre-collision sensing system
suspension stabilizer system

The Lexus GS 450h responds eagerly to all commands from the driver's seat.

Honda

Unlike Toyota, Japanese manufacturer Honda is taking a more measured approach to the development of hybrid vehicles, most likely because it is also busy developing vehicles powered by hydrogen and natural gas. Since its tiny Insight was introduced in December of 1999 as the first modern hybrid car in the United States, it added only two more models, the Civic and Accord Hybrids. Then, in mid-2006, with sales at a trickle, Honda announced it was taking the Insight out of production. However, company spokesman Chris Naughton said Insights would probably still be available, but very scarce, into the fourth quarter of the year. He also said Honda was preparing an all-new, relatively inexpensive hybrid car for sale in 2009. The compact Civic Hybrid was put into production in December of 2001 and updated when the Civic was redesigned for the 2006 model year. The Honda Accord Hybrid, sometimes referred to as a "muscle hybrid," was introduced in December of 2004. Honda's hybrid system,

The redesigned 2006 Honda Civic Hybrid is more powerful and more economical than its predecessor.

The Honda Civic lets the vehicles behind it know that it is a fuel sipper.

The Accord Hybrid is the most powerful Honda sedan.

known as Integrated Motor Assist, places an electric motor between the transmission and gasoline engine in the spot where the flywheel normally would be. While the Insight is more about fuel-economy bragging rights than it is about practicality, the Civic Hybrid demonstrates that a four-door compact sedan can be adapted to highly efficient hybrid power with little penalty. The four-door, front-wheel-drive sedan drives very much like the conventional model.

The Japanese manufacturer took gas-electric power in a different direction when it introduced the Honda Accord Hybrid. The primary function of the electric motor is to boost power—and it makes the front-wheel-drive sedan the most potent Accord in the lineup. Still, the hybrid powerplant emits fewer pollutants and it does get slightly better fuel mileage than its counterpart.

Here is a rundown on the Honda hybrid vehicles.

2006 Honda Insight

Nearly seven years after its introduction, the Insight remains the most fuel-efficient automobile sold in the United States. The EPA rates manual-transmission models at 60 miles per gallon in the city and 66 on the highway. Insights with automatic transmissions are rated at 57 city/56 highway. With room for two people but not much more, the tiny Insight is impractical for most buyers. That no doubt explains why sales declined to the point where Honda decided to take it out of production. But it is adored by a hearty band of enthusiasts who often report fuel mileage that exceeds the EPA estimates. It continues to be a showcase of engineering ingenuity focused wholly on extracting the maximum miles per gallon from a car. The Integrated Motor Assist powertrain, the aerodynamic shape, the extensive use of aluminum, and even the rear-wheel fender skirts and low-rolling-resistance tires make the Insight as efficient as possible.

The Honda Insight was the first modern-era hybrid vehicle sold in the United States when it was introduced in December of 1999.

Nick's Notes: It may come as a surprise to some that this little car is comfortable for two adults, powerful enough to keep up with traffic, and fun to drive. The steering is precise, the brakes are competent, and handling is predictable. Enthusiasts may prefer the manual transmission, but the continuously variable automatic shifter is the more sensible alternative because it manages the mix of gasoline and electric power more effectively, and that keeps the battery from draining excessively. As I drove a manual-transmission Insight on busy highways, in traffic-clogged towns, and on challenging back roads, I was always keenly aware of how small and light the car is. At less than a ton soaking wet, the Insight is easily buffeted by wind and passing tractor-trailers.

From its informative instrument panel to its wind-cheating wheels and rear fender skirts, the Honda Insight is designed to help the driver get the most out of the hybrid driving experience.

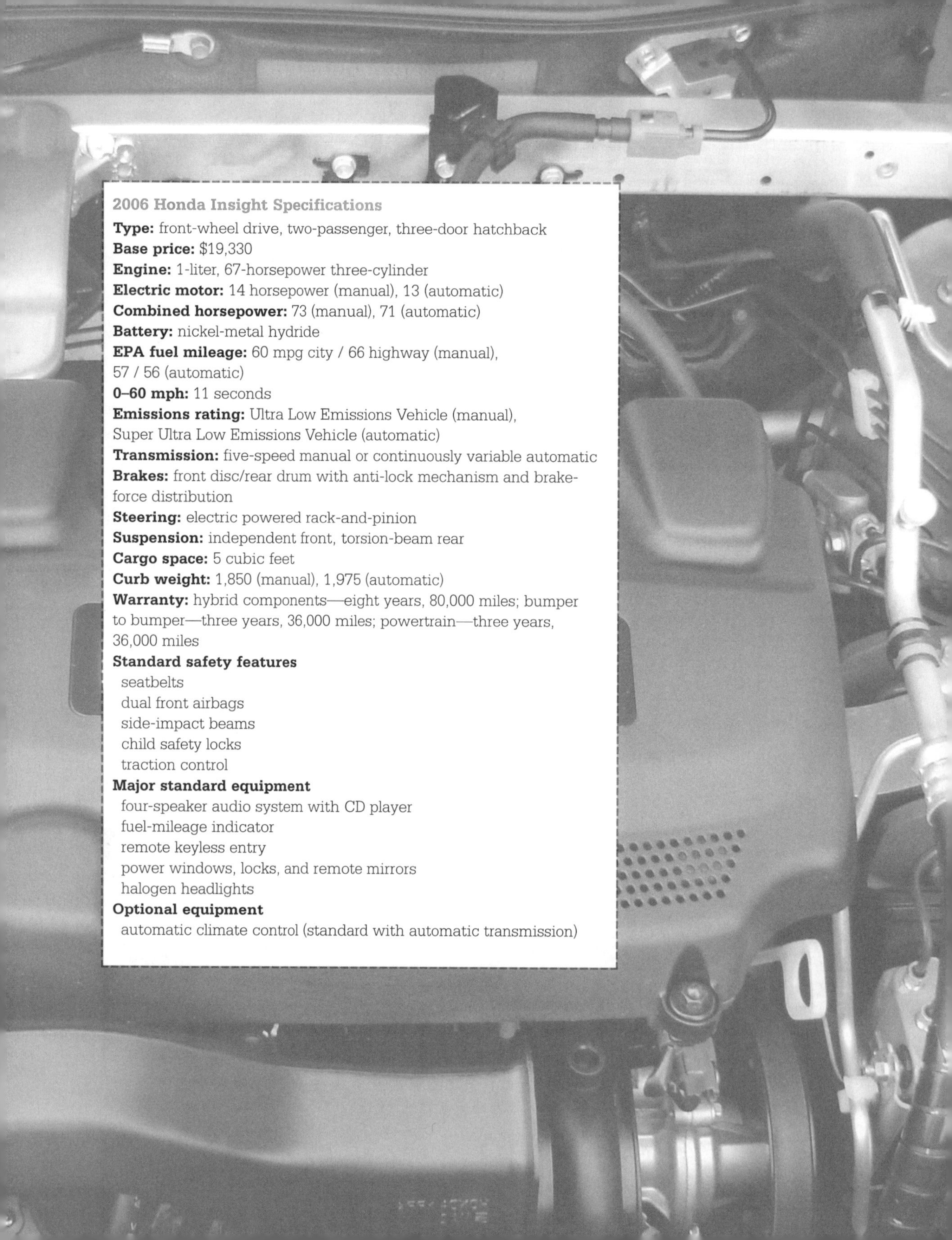

2006 Honda Insight Specifications

Type: front-wheel drive, two-passenger, three-door hatchback

Base price: $19,330

Engine: 1-liter, 67-horsepower three-cylinder

Electric motor: 14 horsepower (manual), 13 (automatic)

Combined horsepower: 73 (manual), 71 (automatic)

Battery: nickel-metal hydride

EPA fuel mileage: 60 mpg city / 66 highway (manual), 57 / 56 (automatic)

0–60 mph: 11 seconds

Emissions rating: Ultra Low Emissions Vehicle (manual), Super Ultra Low Emissions Vehicle (automatic)

Transmission: five-speed manual or continuously variable automatic

Brakes: front disc/rear drum with anti-lock mechanism and brake-force distribution

Steering: electric powered rack-and-pinion

Suspension: independent front, torsion-beam rear

Cargo space: 5 cubic feet

Curb weight: 1,850 (manual), 1,975 (automatic)

Warranty: hybrid components—eight years, 80,000 miles; bumper to bumper—three years, 36,000 miles; powertrain—three years, 36,000 miles

Standard safety features
  seatbelts
  dual front airbags
  side-impact beams
  child safety locks
  traction control

Major standard equipment
  four-speaker audio system with CD player
  fuel-mileage indicator
  remote keyless entry
  power windows, locks, and remote mirrors
  halogen headlights

Optional equipment
  automatic climate control (standard with automatic transmission)

The Honda Insight cabin is comfortable for two adults despite the diminutive dimensions of its exterior.

Honda Civic Hybrid

After surprising the motoring public with the introduction of hybrid power in its purpose-built Insight in 1999, Honda installed a more powerful Integrated Motor Assist powertrain in a 2003 Honda Civic. Not only did the hybrid car look like a standard gasoline-powered model, it pretty much acted like one. Its 93 horsepower was enough; it handled well and had room for four and usable trunk space. Fuel mileage was in the high 40s and it was easy on emissions. It quickly became Honda's top-selling hybrid model.

For the 2006 model year, when the entire Honda Civic lineup was redesigned, the hybrid engineers proved that progress never stands still. They increased power by about 20%, fuel efficiency by a couple of miles per gallon, and managed to make the whole system more compact. They also re-engineered the 1.3-liter, four-cylinder powerplant so it shuts down under deceleration, and they increased the output of the electric motor by 50% without making it any bigger. The Civic Hybrid can now move on its electric motor alone at low speeds with a light load.

The result is a Hybrid sedan that is a mere 75 pounds heavier than a similarly equipped, conventional EX sedan and only a second slower to 60 mph. At 10.4 cubic feet, the trunk is only about 1.5 cubic feet smaller. But there is one big difference. If you believe the EPA, you will get 49 miles per gallon of fuel in the city and 51 on the open road, compared to the EX's 30 city/40 highway. And the hybrid has a better emissions rating.

On the outside, the 2006 Honda Civic Hybrid is almost identical to its traditionally powered counterpart.

Facing page, top to bottom: The gauge on the left tells the driver when the Honda Civic Hybrid is generating or using electrical power. A smooth, continuously variable transmission is the only one available in a Honda Civic Hybrid. The IMA label appears on the Honda Civic Hybrid engine but most of the electric components are somewhere other than under the hood: the electric motor is next to the transmission and the battery pack is behind the rear axle.

Nick's Notes: **My experience in both cars was a bit different, but equally telling. In a week of mixed driving conditions, the hybrid car averaged 42 mpg. In a week of mostly highway driving, the EX sedan averaged 33 mpg. Other than that, the driving experience was quite similar. Both cars handled well, thanks to excellent steering, brakes, and suspension, but the ride was sometimes harsh over uneven road surfaces.**

On the outside, the new design is clean, modern, and handsome—with little more than a badge to separate the two vehicles. Inside, the hybrid sedan is roomy for up to four adults of average size and gets the same top-of-the-line options as the EX sedan, with one exception. It does not come with a sunroof.

Honda Civic Hybrid Specifications

Type: front-wheel drive, four- or five-passenger sedan

Base price: $22,150

Engine: 1.3-liter, 93-horsepower four-cylinder

Electric motor(s): 20 horsepower

Combined horsepower: 110

Battery: nickel-metal hydride

EPA fuel mileage: 49 mpg city / 51 highway

0–60 mph: 11.3 seconds

Emissions rating: Advanced Technology–Partial Zero Emissions Vehicle

Transmission: continuously variable automatic

Brakes: anti-lock front disc/rear drum with brake assist and brake force distribution

Steering: electric powered rack-and-pinion

Suspension: independent at all four wheels

Cargo space: 10.6 cubic feet

Curb weight: 2,875 pounds

Warranty: hybrid components—eight years, 80,000 miles; powertrain—5 years, 60,000 miles; bumper to bumper—three years, 36,000 miles

Standard safety equipment
  driver and front passenger, front and side airbags
  side curtain airbags
  seatbelts
  side-impact door beams
  child-seat anchors
  child safety locks

Major standard features
  halogen headlights
  six-speaker stereophonic sound system
  MP3 player capability with input jack
  automatic climate control
  cruise control
  fuel consumption indicator
  power doors and locks
  power mirrors with integrated turn signals

Major options
  navigation system

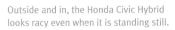

Honda Accord Hybrid

It can get you there faster, go farther on a gallon of gasoline, and be less offensive to the environment. That pretty much sums up the benefits of a Honda Accord Hybrid when it is compared to its conventional, V-6-powered garagemate. On the downside, it will cost a few thousand dollars more.

When Honda introduced its Accord Hybrid to the public for the 2005 model year, it made it clear that the application of its Integrated Motor Assist was not all about fuel economy. This time it was about using the technology to enhance power.

It didn't downsize the engine and then bring back its performance with a powerful electric motor. The V-6 engine is basically the same as the one in the conventional Accord, and the electric motor is rated at only 16 horsepower.

But that's enough to let the hybrid car scoot from a stop to 60 mph in 7.5 seconds, a half second quicker than its counterpart.

For 2006, the horsepower ratings have changed slightly, with the hybrid car rated at 253 horsepower (from 255) and the V-6 sedan rated at 244 horsepower (from 240).

The hybrid car remains marginally quicker than the V-6 sedan, but revised EPA ratings have dropped the average fuel mileage rating from 32 to 28. That's still 5 mpg better than the conventional sedan.

Although IMA is the biggest contributor to fuel efficiency, it is not the only one. The gasoline engine incorporates Variable Cylinder Management (VCM) technology. During cruising, coasting, and braking, VCM deactivates three cylinders. This process involves a lot more than simply cutting back the spark to one cylinder bank. Honda developed electrically powered motor mounts to counteract the inherent roughness in three-cylinder power. It also needed to install an anti-noise system to cancel the booming sound that results from cylinder deactivation.

Another significant difference between the Accord and other Honda hybrids is the transmission. The Accord shuns a continuously variable transmission in favor of a conventional five-speed automatic shifter, which is as smooth and unobtrusive as it is in the gasoline-powered car.

Visually, there is little to separate this car from the manufacturer's top-of-the-line V-6 sedan. On the exterior, the sharp-eyed observer will notice the addition of a small "Hybrid" badge and an unobtrusive spoiler on the trunk lid, a different grille color, and the five-spoke wheels.

Inside, located almost inconspicuously beneath the speedometer, are a fuel-consumption monitor and bar-graph gauges that tell you when the electric motor is assisting and when electricity is being generated. A green "ECO" light flashes on whenever the Hybrid is sipping on three cylinders.

As the top dog in the Accord lineup, the hybrid sedan is equipped with a full complement of luxury features, including leather seats. Fresh-air lovers will be glad to know that a sunroof, unavailable in the early sedans, has been added as a standard feature.

Nick's Notes: **My experience behind the wheel of the Accord Hybrid came in the first model year. I was impressed by the smoothness and the luxury-car-like appointments. The handling was reasonably precise; the ride was controlled but compliant enough to take the sting out of at least some potholes. While the steering responded accurately, I did feel that it could have given a little more feedback on what was happening down where the rubber met the road.**

During my travels, I averaged 27 miles per gallon of regular fuel, which compares with 23 mpg for a 2006 V-6-powered Accord. The difference is significant, but prospective Accord buyers may have second thoughts when they learn that the hybrid Honda has a base price $3,600 higher than its V-6 relative.

Readouts beneath the speedometer record trip distance and miles per gallon in the Honda Accord Hybrid.

The distinctive wheels separate the hybrid model from other Honda Accords.

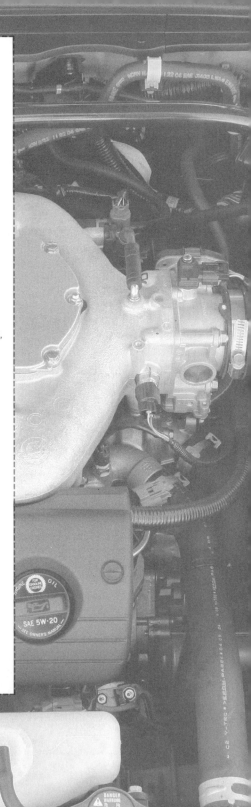

Honda Accord Hybrid Specifications

Type: front-wheel drive, five-passenger sedan

Base price: $30,990

Engine: 3-liter, 240-horsepower V-6

Electric motor(s): 16 horsepower

Combined horsepower: 253

Battery: nickel-metal hydride

EPA fuel mileage: 25 mpg city / 34 highway

0–60 mph: 7.5 seconds

Emissions rating: Advanced Technology–Partial Zero Emissions Vehicle

Transmission: five-speed automatic

Brakes: four-wheel, anti-lock discs with brake assist and brake force distribution

Steering: power rack-and-pinion

Suspension: independent at all four wheels

Cargo space: 11.2 cubic feet

Curb weight: 3,589 pounds

Warranty: hybrid components—eight years, 80,000 miles; powertrain—five years, 60,000 miles; bumper to bumper—three years, 36,000 miles

Standard safety equipment

  driver and front passenger, front and side airbags

  side curtain airbags

  seatbelts

  stability control

  traction control

  side-impact door beams

  child-seat anchors

  child safety locks

Major standard features

  six-speaker stereophonic sound system with six-disc CD changer

  dual-zone automatic climate control

  sunroof

  cruise control

  leather upholstery

  heated front seats

  eight-way power driver's seat

  fuel consumption indicator

  power doors and locks

  heated power mirrors with turn signal indicators

Major options

  navigation system

The speedometer may be a bit optimistic, but the Honda Accord Hybrid has plenty of pep.

A navigation system is optional on the Honda Accord Hybrid.

A small rear spoiler gives the Accord Hybrid an aerodynamic advantage.

With the introduction of the 2005 Ford Escape Hybrid, Ford Motor Company became the first manufacturer to produce a sport-utility vehicle powered by a gasoline engine and an electric motor. The Escape has been followed by the 2006 Mercury Mariner Hybrid—a slightly upscale, near clone to the Escape Hybrid, which arrived a year earlier than expected as a 2006 model.

The Escape Hybrid comes standard with front-wheel drive and offers all-wheel drive as an option. The Mariner Hybrid is available only as an all-wheel-drive vehicle. Both vehicles are full hybrids, which means they can be powered by the gasoline engine and electric motor working together, by the gasoline engine alone, and—under limited circumstances—by the electric motor alone.

The system is similar to one developed earlier by Toyota—and that led to some erroneous speculation that Ford simply had purchased the right to use a slightly modified version of the Japanese powertrain. Representatives of both companies have said that is not true and have affirmed that Toyota offered no technical assistance to Ford. Said Deep, a Ford spokesman, noted that, "The way we use our systems is entirely different than theirs." However, Ford purchases its transaxles from a Japanese firm owned by Toyota, and Sanyo—a Japanese electronics giant—supplies the battery packs.

A Mercury Mariner was the only hybrid vehicle available for testing as this book was being written, but because it's nearly identical to the Ford Escape Hybrid, my observations will cover both. However, the specifications for the two are slightly different because the Mercury is a bit more upscale.

An independent suspension setup at all four wheels gives the Ford Escape Hybrid a comfortable ride.

More than eight inches of ground clearance allow the Ford Escape hybrid to travel off-road.

Top: The Ford Escape Hybrid can be outfitted for weekend and vacation adventures.

Bottom: Astute observers will note that the taillights and front end of the Mercury Mariner distinguish it from the Ford Escape.

Mercury Mariner Hybrid/Ford Escape Hybrid

For motorists who live in or near urban areas, one of these hybrid twins may be exactly the right answer. Not only does their powertrain return better fuel mileage in the city than it does on the highway, the Escape and Mariner are categorized as small sport-utility vehicles. As a result, they are more maneuverable and easier to park than their larger competitors. But don't let the size fool you. Inside, they are capable of carrying up to 62 cubic feet of cargo. You can use these vehicles for a run to the home improvement center, even if it is located in center city. Should you seek solace from the din of downtown, you can use a Mariner Hybrid or similarly equipped Ford Escape for that camping vacation or hunting trip. These two, with 8.4 inches of ground clearance, are the only hybrid SUVs authorized for off-road use. There is one exception: Ford also sells a front-wheel-drive Ford Escape Hybrid, and it is best-suited for on-road travel.

Viewed from the side, the Mercury Mariner Hybrid, above, and the Ford Escape Hybrid are nearly identical.

Nick's Notes: The 155 horsepower available in all of these vehicles is adequate, if not exhilarating. They are not greased lightning from a standstill, but there is plenty of energy available for passing slowpokes and merging onto freeways. I could not match the Mariner's EPA fuel rating, but I did manage to average almost 27 miles per gallon in a week of mostly gentle driving.

The steering is responsive, the brakes are strong enough to handle a nearly two-ton vehicle, and the suspension offers a reasonably comfortable ride on paved surfaces. Small or not, the SUV twins offer that commanding view from the captain's chair that SUV buyers love.

There is one idiosyncrasy not common to most other hybrids. When the engine shuts down at a traffic signal, the air conditioner normally stops running, too. However, this can be overcome by setting it to "max" or turning on the defroster.

The different grilles give the two vehicles a distinctively different look when viewed head-on, but the distinction blurs when these four-door SUVs are seen from the side. The overall design is not trendsetting, but it's certainly not offensive.

Inside, materials are of acceptable quality, and gauges and switches are logically placed. The seats are adequate and the cabin is quiet. In the final analysis, Ford and Mercury have less expensive and more versatile vehicles than their only current competitors: the Toyota Highlander and Lexus RX 400h.

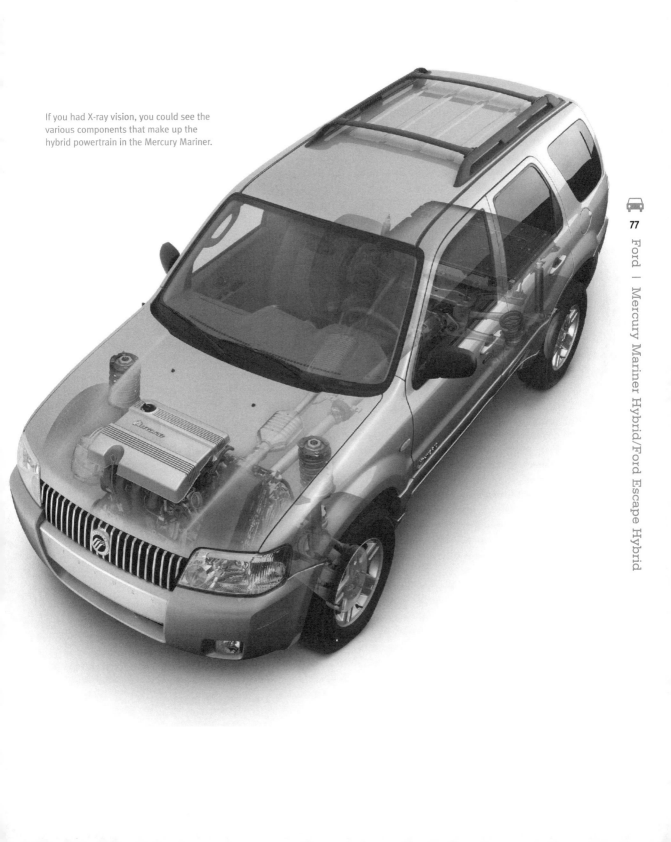

If you had X-ray vision, you could see the various components that make up the hybrid powertrain in the Mercury Mariner.

Mercury Mariner Hybrid Specifications

Type: five-passenger, all-wheel-drive sport-utility vehicle

Base price: $29,225

Engine: 2.3-liter, 133-horsepower four-cylinder

Electric motor(s): 94 horsepower

Combined horsepower: 155

Battery: nickel-metal hydride

EPA fuel mileage: 33 mpg city / 29 highway

0–60 mph: 11 seconds

Emissions rating: Advanced Technology–Partial Zero Emissions Vehicle

Transmission: continuously variable automatic

Brakes: four-wheel, anti-lock discs

Steering: electrically operated rack-and-pinion

Suspension: independent at all four wheels

Cargo space: 27.6–65.6 cubic feet

Curb weight: 3,787 pounds

Warranty: hybrid components—eight years, 100,000 miles; bumper to bumper—three years, 36,000 miles

Standard safety equipment
  driver and front passenger, front airbags
  seatbelts
  side-impact door beams
  child-seat anchors

Optional safety equipment
  side curtain airbags
  rollover sensor
  driver and front passenger, side airbags

Major standard features
  four-speaker audio system with six-disc CD changer
  air-conditioning
  power windows and door locks
  cruise control
  six-way power driver's seat
  60/40 split fold-down rear seat
  multi-function message center
  wood-grained, chrome, and satin finish on interior
  leather-wrapped steering wheel
  tire pressure monitor
  automatic dimming rear-view mirror
  roof rack
  fog lights

Major options
  navigation system
  premium seven-speaker audio system with six-CD changer
  sunroof
  leather upholstery
  heated front seats
  heated outside mirrors

Viewed from almost any vantage point, the Mercury Mariner Hybrid is an attractive blend of form and function.

Ford Escape Hybrid Specifications

Type: five-passenger sport-utility vehicle

Base price: $26,900 (FWD), $28,525 (AWD)

Engine: 2.3-liter, 133-horsepower four-cylinder

Electric motor(s): 94 horsepower

Combined horsepower: 155

Battery: nickel-metal hydride

EPA fuel mileage: 36 mpg city / 31 highway (FWD), 33 / 29 (AWD)

0–60 mph: 11 seconds

Emissions rating: Advanced Technology–Partial Zero Emissions Vehicle

Transmission: continuously variable automatic

Brakes: four-wheel, anti-lock discs

Steering: electrically operated rack-and-pinion

Suspension: independent at all four wheels

Cargo space: 27.6–65.6 cubic feet

Curb weight: 3,610 pounds (FWD), 3,775 (AWD)

Warranty: hybrid components–eight years, 100,000 miles; bumper to bumper–three years, 36,000 miles

Standard safety equipment
  driver and front passenger, front airbags
  seatbelts
  side-impact door beams
  child-seat anchors

Optional safety equipment
  side curtain airbags
  rollover sensor
  driver and front passenger, side airbags

Major standard features
  four-speaker audio system with six-disc CD changer
  air-conditioning
  power windows, door locks, and mirrors
  keyless entry
  cruise control
  six-way power driver's seat
  60/40 split fold-down rear seat
  multi-function message center
  roof rack
  fog lights

Major options
  navigation system
  premium seven-speaker audio system with six-CD changer
  sunroof
  leather upholstery
  heated front seats
  heated outside mirrors

Inside and out, the Ford Escape Hybrid is a picture of practicality. The Ford Escape Hybrid battery pack is stowed safely beneath the sport-utility vehicle's cargo compartment (right). The gauge to the left of the instrument panel signals when electrical power is being used and when it is being generated.

A Buyer's Guide to Hybrids

General Motors has announced the joint development of a two-mode hybrid system with DaimlerChrysler and BMW that will eventually appear on a variety of vehicles, starting in 2007. For 2006, the company offers only a mild hybrid system on two pickup trucks and a slightly more sophisticated system on its Saturn Vue Green Line sport-utility vehicle.

The hybrid trucks, Chevrolet Silverado and GMC Sierra extended cab pickups, have an electric motor sandwiched between the engine and transmission. It does not contribute power for moving the vehicles. Instead, it acts as a starter so that the trucks' engines can shut down at traffic signals and restart automatically when the driver's foot returns to the accelerator. It also acts as a generator during coasting and braking to keep the 42-volt battery pack properly charged. Extra fuel savings come from fuel shut-off to the cylinders any time the truck is coasting or braking.

The Saturn Vue Green Line Hybrid puts an electric motor between a 2.4-liter, four-cylinder engine and the vehicle's four-speed automatic transmission. In addition to performing the same functions as the motor in the pickup trucks, it provides additional power during launch and gives the gasoline engine a boost when it is under full acceleration.

The Chevrolet Silverado hybrid pickup truck is every bit as rugged as its standard-engine counterpart.

Drivers of the Chevrolet Silverado pickup truck can expect up to a 10 percent increase in fuel efficiency when they opt for the hybrid model.

Chevrolet Silverado Hybrid/GMC Sierra Hybrid

Although the hybrid system in these pickup trucks reduces fuel consumption only by an estimated 10%, it in no way affects the vehicles' functionality. The 5.3-liter, 295-horsepower V-8 engine is the same one used in the conventional pickups, so towing capacity, load limits, and grade climbing are unaffected.

In addition, the system has a bonus application, particularly for buyers who will use it as a work truck. In addition to replenishing the battery pack and powering onboard systems, the starter-generator can supply electricity to the truck's four outlets for the operation of power tools or laptop computers. The 120-volt system can even run household appliances during a power outage, from the outlets located in the cabin and at the rear of the pickup bed. And there's no need to worry about draining the batteries. Push and hold the power outlet button and everything will shut down but the engine. It can keep the generator going for up to 32 hours, and the horn will sound when fuel is running low.

An electrically driven hydraulic pump keeps the heating or air-conditioning operating when the engine shuts down in traffic. All other items, such as lights and the radio, get their juice from the vehicles' conventional 12-volt battery.

One note of caution: the auto off/on feature at traffic stops can be a bit disconcerting to new drivers because the trucks will drift backward during start-up on an incline—just as they would if the vehicles had a manual transmission. This can be averted two ways: keep the left foot on the brake until the right foot hits the accelerator and the gasoline engine restarts; defeat the idle-stop feature by pushing the tow-haul button.

Nick's Notes: I did not have the opportunity to give the hybrid pickup truck a full test, but others who did reported that the government's fuel economy estimates are optimistic. The four-wheel-drive trucks generally averaged between 14 and 16 miles per gallon of gasoline, depending on their use, but that still is an approximate 10% gain over the consumption of conventional vehicles in similar circumstances.

Expect for a change of badges, the GMC Sierra hybrid pickup truck is a carbon copy of the Chevrolet Silverado.

Because of its ability to generate electricity, the Chevrolet Silverado hybrid pickup truck has 120-volt outlets that can supply power for a variety of devices, including household appliances during a blackout.

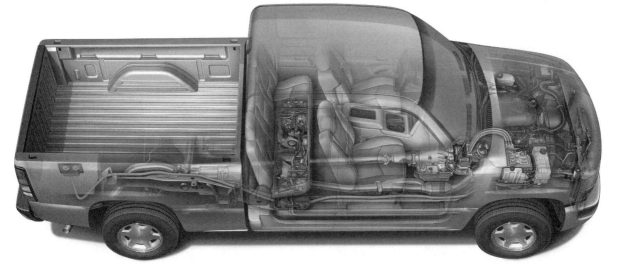

A mild hybrid, the GMC Sierra pickup truck has the same V-8 powertrain as a conventional Sierra.

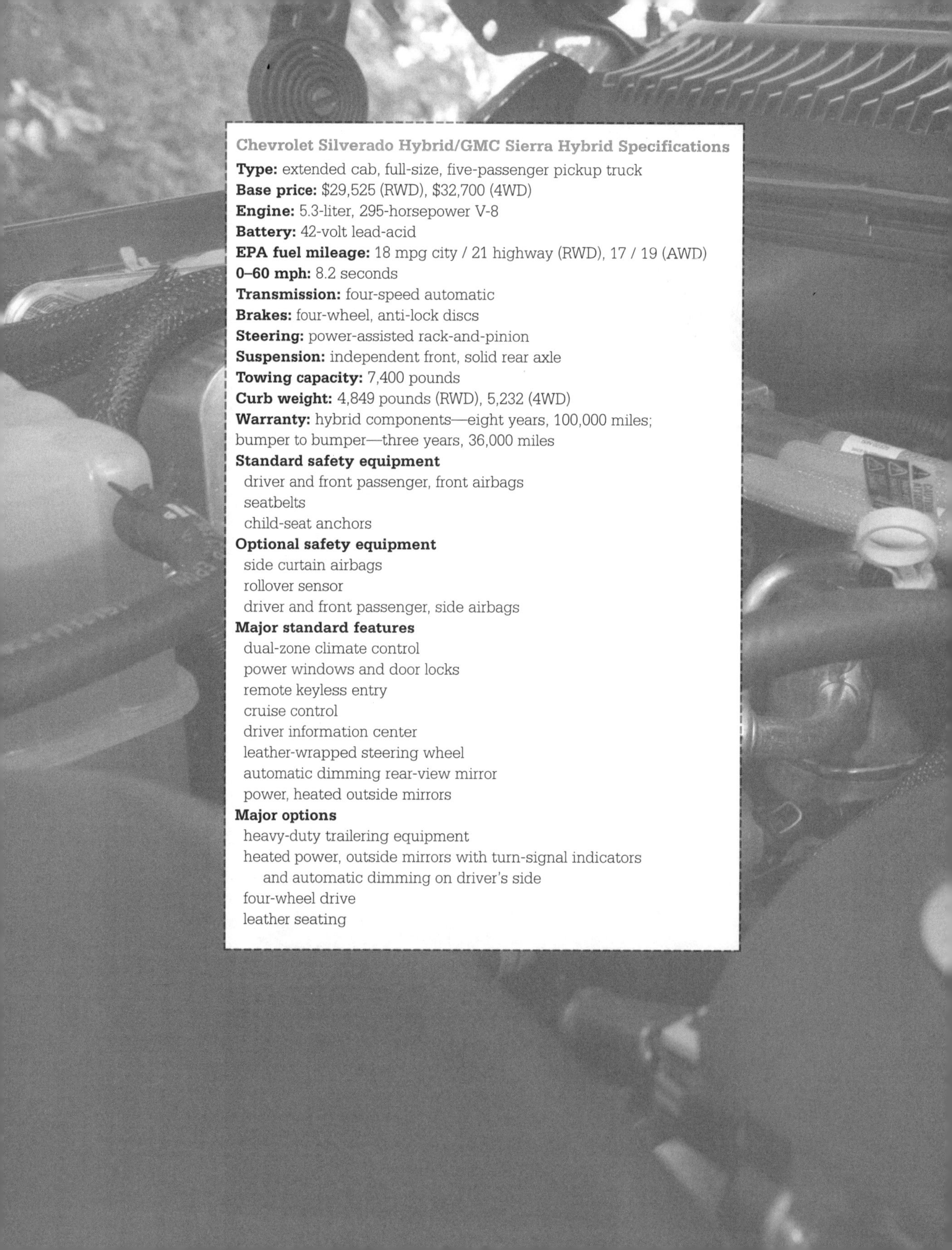

Chevrolet Silverado Hybrid/GMC Sierra Hybrid Specifications

Type: extended cab, full-size, five-passenger pickup truck
Base price: $29,525 (RWD), $32,700 (4WD)
Engine: 5.3-liter, 295-horsepower V-8
Battery: 42-volt lead-acid
EPA fuel mileage: 18 mpg city / 21 highway (RWD), 17 / 19 (AWD)
0–60 mph: 8.2 seconds
Transmission: four-speed automatic
Brakes: four-wheel, anti-lock discs
Steering: power-assisted rack-and-pinion
Suspension: independent front, solid rear axle
Towing capacity: 7,400 pounds
Curb weight: 4,849 pounds (RWD), 5,232 (4WD)
Warranty: hybrid components—eight years, 100,000 miles; bumper to bumper—three years, 36,000 miles

Standard safety equipment
  driver and front passenger, front airbags
  seatbelts
  child-seat anchors

Optional safety equipment
  side curtain airbags
  rollover sensor
  driver and front passenger, side airbags

Major standard features
  dual-zone climate control
  power windows and door locks
  remote keyless entry
  cruise control
  driver information center
  leather-wrapped steering wheel
  automatic dimming rear-view mirror
  power, heated outside mirrors

Major options
  heavy-duty trailering equipment
  heated power, outside mirrors with turn-signal indicators
    and automatic dimming on driver's side
  four-wheel drive
  leather seating

The full-size GMC Sierra, above, and
Chevrolet Silverado hybrid pickup trucks all
have extended cabs that give them five-
passenger capability.

Saturn VUE Green Line Hybrid

Saturn executives believe the VUE Green Line hybrid sport-utility vehicle has one major advantage over its hybrid competition: price. Even though the hybrid system adds approximately $1,500 to the cost of the vehicle, its base price is $22,995.

The VUE Green Line, which went on sale in late summer of 2006, uses a 170-horsepower, 2.4-liter, four-cylinder engine and an electric motor that primarily assists acceleration. That's 27 more horses than the conventional 2.2-liter, four-cylinder engine in the base front-wheel-drive VUE. The hybrid system increases fuel efficiency and reduces pollution four ways: engine shut off at temporary stops, fuel cutoff during deceleration, electric motor assist to the gasoline engine during acceleration, and the capture of electricity when the motor converts to a generator during braking. Fuel economy has been estimated at 27 miles per gallon in the city and 32 on the highway. This compares with the 22 city/27 highway estimate for a comparably equipped vehicle with the 2.2-liter gasoline engine.

There are several reasons why Saturn has been able to produce its hybrid more cheaply than similar offerings from Toyota and Ford. It does not offer the

Nick's Notes: The hybrid VUE had not been released for evaluation as this book was written, so I had no opportunity to test it. However, the staff at *AutoWeek* spent a short time with it and "found it promises a lot for the mainstream customer who needs to combine utility, an affordable sticker (price) and reasonable fuel economy."

With its rear hatchback and generous cargo space, the Saturn VUE Green Line is every bit as practical as the standard VUE sport-utility vehicle.

option of four-wheel drive. The electric motor cannot propel the vehicle by itself for more than a few seconds, so Saturn did not have to re-engineer the existing powertrain. And the VUE's electric motor is combined with the vehicle's alternator—a simpler setup than Toyota's use of motors and a complicated gear arrangement to coordinate the power sources.

All Saturn VUEs were mildly redesigned for the 2006 model year. At the front end there is a new hood, grille, and headlights. At the rear, there is a new step pad. Inside, the center of the VUE's dashboard and the center console have been redesigned to increase storage space. There is a rear cargo organizer that holds grocery bags and side storage bins that can hold additional cargo.

All Saturn VUE sport-utility vehicles were mildly redesigned for the 2006 model year. But only the Green Line, with hybrid power, has a gauge to tell you when its battery is charging and when its electric motor is providing power during acceleration.

Saturn VUE Green Line Hybrid Specifications

Type: five-passenger, front-wheel-drive sport-utility vehicle
Base price: $23,000 (estimated)
Engine: 2.4-liter, 170-horsepower four-cylinder
Electric motor(s): power rating not available
Battery: nickel-metal hydride
EPA fuel mileage: 27 mpg city / 32 highway (estimated)
0–60 mph: 10.2 seconds
Emissions rating: not available
Transmission: four-speed automatic
Brakes: anti-lock front disc/rear drum with traction control
Steering: electrically operated rack-and-pinion
Suspension: independent at all four wheels
Cargo space: 30.8 cubic feet
Curb weight: 3,474 pounds
Warranty: hybrid components—eight years, 100,000 miles;
bumper to bumper—three years, 36,000 miles
Standard safety equipment
  driver and front passenger, front airbags
  seatbelts
  side-impact door beams
Optional safety equipment
  side curtain airbags
Major standard features
  cruise control
  power windows and door locks
  power mirrors
  remote keyless entry
  air-conditioning
  stereophonic sound system with CD player
Major options
  rear seat entertainment system
  leather seats
  six-way power driver's seat
  heated front seats
  sunroof
  six-speaker premium sound system with MP3 player

The Saturn VUE Green Line has a simpler, less expensive powertrain than the full hybrids from Toyota and Ford.

The angular exterior design serves to emphasize the pure practicality of the Saturn VUE Green Line.

03:

{Future Hybrids,
Alternative-Fuel Vehicles,
and Super-efficient
Small Cars}

Hyundai Accent

{Future Hybrids, Alternative-Fuel Vehicles, and Super-efficient Small Cars}

Everyone associated with the automotive industry seems to agree on one thing: something must be done to curb the world's huge and growing demand for oil. With 15 million or more cars and light trucks sold in the United States annually—and with the number climbing quickly in China, India, and other less-developed parts of the world— the demand for fuel will only continue to grow, and the supply will only diminish.

Future Gasoline-Electric Hybrids

Right now, the gasoline-electric hybrid vehicle seems to provide one quick and relatively easy way to tame, at least slightly, the country's unquenchable thirst for gasoline. While the technology is complicated, its application is basically seamless to the vehicle's owners. Hybrid cars drive almost identically to conventional ones, the service routines are basically unchanged, and the existing gas station network can provide the fuel. From an automaker's point of view, hybrid power-plants can be integrated into vehicle assembly lines without major disruption to the manufacturing process.

Balanced against that, of course, are the facts that hybrid cars cost thousands of dollars more than their traditional counterparts and require heavy and cumbersome battery packs that steal valuable cargo space and slightly disrupt the vehicle's balance.

Major manufacturers seem to agree that hydrogen is the fuel of the future, and they have already put a lot of time, money, and energy into developing hydrogen-powered automobiles that are being tested in the United States, Europe, and Japan. But they recognize that there are major hurdles to overcome before hydrogen fuel can be integrated into the automotive mainstream. How can it be made affordable? How can it be proven safe enough to satisfy buyers? How can it be conveniently distributed? The answers are coming, they say, but could be ten to twenty years away.

All of this has left much of the industry in a quandary. Many decision makers simply cannot determine if hybrid vehicles will gain wide public acceptance, or for how long. When gas prices spike dramatically, there is a rush for hybrids. When they decline, American motorists slip right back into their gas-guzzling ways.

"The interest goes way up when gas prices go up," said Wade Hoyt, public affairs manager for Toyota, the world's leading manufacturer of hybrid vehicles. "Then it slacks off when prices go down. It's hard to cite statistics, though, because we sell every hybrid vehicle we get into the United States."

In May of 2006, after gasoline prices had settled in around $3 a gallon for several months, combined sales of hybrids totaled a record 23,554 units. However, hybrids still represented only 1.6% of light-duty vehicle sales.

As a result, many of the manufacturers are proceeding with caution, slowly moving ahead with the development of hybrid vehicles while at the same time keeping their options open. Even Toyota is investigating and testing alternative fuel and hydrogen fuel cells. Here's a rundown of what the major car manufacturers are planning—and what role hybrids play in their view of the future.

General Motors

Elizabeth A. Lowery, General Motors vice president for environment and energy, says GM is taking a cautious approach to the emerging technology. "It's an interesting time for hybrids," she said. "We will have to see what the market will bear . . . if all the technologies being developed are what the consumer wants."

She noted that General Motors has several hybrid vehicles for sale now, and has several more in the works. One General Motors program is to build a hybrid that saves fuel, but does not incorporate all of the technology of full hybrids. Mild hybrid systems make the vehicles more affordable. A second program is the two-mode hybrid, which is being developed in a joint program with Daimler-Chrysler and BMW. The two-mode system, which employs electric motors inside the transmission, decreases fuel consumption by an estimated 25% and is compatible with small or large vehicles and front-wheel drive, rear-wheel drive, or all-wheel drive. Lowery said that General Motors will initially apply the two-mode technology to sport-utility vehicles.

Lowery also said GM is aggressively pursuing the use of ethanol and has been touting it in the corporation's Live Green, Go Yellow campaign. She noted that there are 1.5 million GM flex-fuel vehicles on the road that can burn gasoline alone or burn E85, a blend that contains 15% gasoline and 85% alcohol distilled from corn. In 2006, she said, GM was scheduled to produce an additional 400,000 flex-fuel vehicles.

Chief Executive Officer Rick Wagoner is a strong ethanol booster, too. He drives a flex-fuel car along with hundreds of Detroit-area GM executives who are required by their employer to fill their cars with E85 whenever it is available.

But Wagoner believes it also is important for General Motors to produce hybrid vehicles, and he has said, "I like our emerging position." Nevertheless, he, too, thinks there is a limit to how many can be sold.

Meanwhile, Lowery said, the corporation is also looking at biodiesel, the renewable fuel that works in diesel engines, "but we have some concern with emissions." She said it is also conducting a demonstration project with hydrogen-powered vehicles.

Hybrids on the horizon. The **Chevrolet Tahoe** and **GMC Yukon** sport-utility vehicles will have a two-mode hybrid powertrain in 2007. The **Cadillac Escalade**, redesigned for the 2006 model year, will have a two-mode hybrid powerplant in 2008. A mild-hybrid powertrain, similar to the one in the Saturn Vue Green Line, will be introduced in 2007 on the **Chevrolet Malibu** and the **Saturn Aura**, a sedan new to the brand.

Ford

Nine months after pledging a major commitment to the development of hybrid cars—250,000 a year by 2010—Ford Motor Co. disclosed a wider strategy to increase fuel efficiency and reduce pollution in all its vehicles.

William Clay Ford Jr., chairman and chief executive, told employees in June of 2006 the hybrid vehicle target was "too narrow to achieve our larger goals." As a result, the company will spend $1.37 billion to set up a center in Gothenburg, Sweden that will be responsible for developing hybrid systems for Volvo, a Ford subsidiary, that can also be adapted for use by Ford of Europe and the Ford Premier Automotive Group. The team at the Swedish center will work closely with Ford's hybrid development team in Detroit.

Ford will also spend $1.8 billion over the next six years in Britain on projects to improve the efficiency of traditional gasoline and diesel engines and lower the weight of its vehicles. The new technologies will be employed in European Ford brands, which include Volvo, Jaguar, and Land Rover.

Ford spokesman Said Deep emphasized that the automotive manufacturer's "commitment to hybrid vehicles has not changed in any way. We are working on third-generation (components) for hybrid vehicles beyond 2008. . . . The only change will be in the mix of technologies."

He said the company expects to expand its line of diesel-powered vehicles in the United States "when we can sell them in all 50 states." The Environmental Protection Agency mandated the use of low-sulfur fuels beginning in 2006 for highway diesel fuel, and 2007 for nonroad diesel fuel. These fuels will enable the use of after-treatment technologies, beginning in 2007, which can reduce harmful emissions by 90 percent or more.

Deep added that alternative fuels are also being explored, noting that the company is producing flexible-fuel cars that can operate on gasoline or ethanol. Already, he noted, there are 1.6 million Ford, Lincoln, and Mercury flex-fuel vehicles on the road. He looks forward to the day when the company will have a hybrid vehicle that burns ethanol.

Hybrids on the horizon. Using a powerplant identical to the one in the Ford Escape and Mercury Mariner, Ford subsidiary Mazda will introduce a hybrid **Mazda Tribute** sport-utility vehicle in 2007. The mid-size **Ford Fusion** and **Mercury Milan** will have a hybrid powertrain in 2008. Under consideration for hybrid power beyond 2008 are the **Ford Edge** mid-size crossover vehicle, the **Ford 500** and **Mercury Montego** sedans, and the **Lincoln MKX,** a replacement for the Aviator sport-utility vehicle.

Chrysler

Nicholas Cappa, advanced technology communications manager for the Chrysler division of DaimlerChrysler, said his company—along with parent Mercedes-Benz, General Motors, and BMW—is moving forward with the two-mode hybrid system. It will first appear in 2008 in the Dodge Durango sport-utility vehicle. Although none had been announced as of summer 2006, "there will be other [hybrid] products," Cappa assured.

Cappa confirmed that, like other manufacturers, Chrysler is working on the development of alternative fuel and hydrogen vehicles. He also said some Chrysler 300 sedans with diesel engines are being tested, but there are no plans now to sell them in the United States. Meanwhile, Chrysler has announced it will sell a Jeep Grand Cherokee sport-utility vehicle with diesel power in the United States starting in 2007, but that it is withdrawing the diesel option from its smaller Liberty sport-utility vehicle.

Hybrids on the horizon. The **Dodge Durango** sport-utility vehicle will have a two-mode hybrid system in 2008.

Nissan

Carlos Ghosn, chief executive officer of Japanese manufacturer Nissan and French automaker Renault, offered his appraisal of hybrids in a talk at an industry/press breakfast preceding the opening of the 2006 New York International Auto Show. "There is a need to diversify away from oil . . . very fast," he readily acknowledged. "But I'm less of a one-solution man. Even though hybrid is one option, it is not the only option."

Ghosn, the man credited with breathing life back into a failing Nissan, sees ethanol, a blend of gasoline and ethyl alcohol produced from plants and plant waste, as a potentially viable option in the United States. "You can substitute it very fast and you don't need to adapt engines. All you need is land and sun and you can make it in your own ground."

Ghosn also sees clean-burning diesel engines as an interim solution since they are more fuel efficient than gasoline engines. And he, too, sees hydrogen down the road. "We're working on fuel cells. It may be five, ten years, but don't underestimate how fast we can move. Yes, there are many solutions. We are working on all of them."

Hybrids on the horizon. The Japanese manufacturer's first hybrid automobile, the **Nissan Altima**, will be on sale in 2007, but only in the eight states that have the most stringent environmental regulations: California, New York, Massachusetts, Connecticut, Vermont, Rhode Island, Maine, and New Jersey. It will team a 2.4-liter, 170-horsepower gasoline engine with an electric motor and employ a continuously variable transmission. The hybrid technology has been purchased from Toyota.

Toyota

Dave Hermance, Toyota's executive engineer for advanced automotive technologies, stands squarely behind hybrid technology and its future. He confirmed that the world's largest producer of hybrid vehicles expects to produce one million annually by about 2012, with 600,000 of them to be sold in the United States. As the technology improves, he said, "The goal is to take half the extra cost out of the hybrid engine. However, the high-voltage battery and the power electronics mean there will always be some incremental costs." Hermance didn't want to talk specifics, but the price premium for a hybrid vehicle has been estimated at $3,000 to $5,000. A 50% cut would reduce the increase to $1,500 to $2,500.

While Toyota continues to investigate all alternative fuels—including hydrogen—Hermance believes "the fuel of the future will be some sort of renewable liquid. Liquid fuels have a lot more energy." Hybrid powertrains, he added, can be adapted to use all types of fuel.

Hybrids on the horizon. The **Lexus LS 600h**, a hybrid-powered version of Toyota's premium brand flagship, will be in dealerships in 2007. As of this writing, no announcements had been made for more hybrid-powered Toyotas, but speculation has centered around the Sienna minivan and the RAV4 sport-utility vehicle.

The hybrid-powered Lexus LS 600h goes on sale in 2007.

Honda

Honda, the second biggest manufacturer of hybrid vehicles sold in the United States, announced in mid-2006 that it was planning to cease production of its slow-selling, two-seat Insight. It was predictably tight-lipped about its future hybrid plans, but company spokesman Chris Naughton did confirm that an all-new hybrid automobile will be added to the Japanese manufacturer's lineup.

Meanwhile, Honda is also moving ahead with diesel-powered cars. It already has natural-gas-powered cars in the hands of customers and a fleet of hydrogen-powered cars on the road.

Hybrids on the horizon. A new hybrid vehicle is expected in 2009, but the company provided only a few details. It will not be based on any existing car. It will be less expensive than the Honda Civic Hybrid and the company expects to produce 200,000 a year, 100,000 for the United States.

Saab

This European division of General Motors has confirmed that it is working on gasoline-electric hybrid cars. Saab Managing Director Jan-Ake Jonsson said, "We are part of the development process . . . [Hybrids] fit into the image of the brand." He has also confirmed that Saab is working on a hybrid powerplant with an engine capable of using E85 ethanol, but did not say when it would be in production.

Hybrids on the horizon. The Swedish manufacturer is working on hybrid power for the **Saab 9-3** and **Saab 9-5** vehicles. The Saab 9-5 is due to be updated in 2007 and the next-generation 9-3 is scheduled for 2008. "We want to put it [hybrid power] on something new that comes out," said Jonsson. "That way we can maximize the potential of the technology."

Diesel Power—from the Europeans

The German manufacturers are investigating or developing gasoline-electric hybrid vehicles, but their primary emphasis appears to be on producing diesel-powered cars for the United States that will be approved for sale in all fifty states. New U.S. regulations mandating cleaner-burning, low-sulfur diesel fuel are expected to make that goal attainable.

Mercedes-Benz

"Today's diesels have better performance and they can match or beat the fuel mileage of many hybrids," said Michelle Murad, product and technology specialist for German manufacturer Mercedes-Benz.

However, she said, the German manufacturer is also moving ahead with the development of hybrid cars in collaboration with General Motors and BMW.

She noted that Mercedes has showcased a few diesel-electric hybrid cars at auto shows in Germany and the United States, "but we have not announced anything. We're working on hybrid technology. If it makes sense at a later time, we will introduce it."

Mercedes-Benz has long been one of the premier manufacturers of diesel-powered cars.

Hybrids on the horizon. A two-mode hybrid system is being developed for Mercedes-Benz vehicles, but in mid-2006 the manufacturer had not announced a timetable or any specific models.

BMW

Like its two partners, BMW is planning to incorporate the two-hybrid system into some of its vehicles. "We have no dedicated date," said Andreas Klugescheid, technology communications manager. "We will phase in the technology over the next three to five years." He did not indicate what models BMW believes would be best suited for the two-mode hybrid.

Klugescheid indicated that BMW's attitude toward diesel-powered cars is pretty much the same as that of other European manufacturers. "When it comes to diesels, we like them. We see a market in the U.S. But we will only market them if they are approved for sale by all fifty states."

Hybrids on the horizon. Like Mercedes-Benz, BMW will have hybrid power, but in mid-2006 it had not disclosed which vehicles or when they will be introduced.

BMW's Turbosteamer

They call it the Turbosteamer and it's an entirely different kind of hybrid powertrain developed by engineers of German manufacturer BMW. True to its name, this system relies on steam to generate an alternate source of power.

With interconnecting piping and other components, the system uses heat from the exhaust and cooling systems to create steam that is used to run what are essentially two steam engines. These engines contribute about 13 horsepower to a 1.8-liter, four-cylinder engine and increase fuel efficiency by about 15%.

There is a lot of complicated science involved, and the Turbosteamer apparatus adds about 200 pounds to the weight of the car. Development continues, but BMW doesn't expect to see it in production until after 2010 at the earliest.

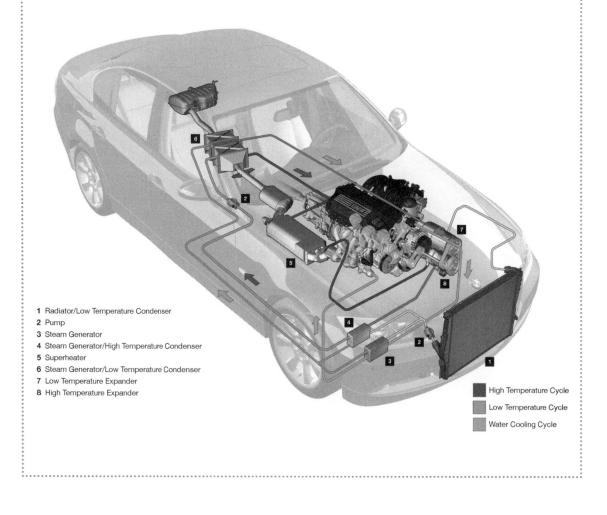

1 Radiator/Low Temperature Condenser
2 Pump
3 Steam Generator
4 Steam Generator/High Temperature Condenser
5 Superheater
6 Steam Generator/Low Temperature Condenser
7 Low Temperature Expander
8 High Temperature Expander

High Temperature Cycle
Low Temperature Cycle
Water Cooling Cycle

Volkswagen

Steve Keyes, director of corporate communications for Volkswagen of America, acknowledged that, "Yes, we are working on hybrid, gasoline-electric as well as diesel-electric vehicles. Our company believes that diesel-electric might well be the ideal combination." He acknowledged that Volkswagen is working with Audi and Porsche to develop a gas-electric hybrid version of its Touareg sport-utility vehicle, but said no date for production has been set.

In the short term, however, he said, "We are still focusing on diesel fuels. We will be introducing a new diesel engine that will be more powerful and will meet the upgraded U.S. standards for diesel fuel. We will have an '08 model that can be sold in all fifty states." He indicated that it would be a Volkswagen Jetta.

Hybrids on the horizon. The **Volkswagen Touareg** sport-utility vehicle will have a hybrid powerplant, but the company did not say when it will be introduced.

Audi

Audi officials have confirmed that the German manufacturer is developing a production version of the hybrid Audi Q7 it displayed at the 2005 Frankfurt Auto Show.

Nevertheless, Filip G. Brabec, product planning manager for German manufacturer Audi, a division of Volkswagen, emphasized that, "Diesel seems like a better option for us. It's definitely something we want to pursue further. We want to see if we can get the most efficiency out of diesel engines."

Brabec said he believes U.S. regulations requiring a 97% reduction in the sulfur content of diesel fuel will make it possible for Audi to bring diesel-powered vehicles into all fifty states.

Hybrids on the horizon. The **Audi Q7** luxury sport-utility vehicle with hybrid power will be sold in 2008. It will combine electric power with a V-8 engine and is expected to consume 13% less fuel than a Q7 with a standard V-8 engine.

Porsche

Bernd Harling, general manager of public relations for German sports-car manufacturer Porsche, also confirmed that, "We are together with VW and Audi in the development of a hybrid—in our case, the Cayenne. It will be within this decade."

As to Porsche's expensive sports cars, Harling did not see a hybrid application for those vehicles.

Hybrids on the horizon. No date for production was announced, but Porsche said it will produce a **Porsche Cayenne** with hybrid power by the end of the decade.

Volvo

Although Volvo parent Ford Motor Co. has announced that it will establish a hybrid development center in Gothenburg, Sweden, Volvo has not announced the development of any specific vehicles.

The Swedish carmaker did say that, in addition to hybrids, the center will focus on the development of alternative fuel vehicles and cleaner, more efficient diesel engines.

Earlier, Dan Johnston, product communications manager, had emphasized the company's commitment to diesels. "We will not have anything [hybrid] for at least a couple of years," Johnston said. "At this point we believe diesels are a good solution."

Volvo spokesman James Hope said the company "is working diligently toward bringing diesel-powered vehicles to the United States by 2009 or 2010."

Hybrids on the horizon. None as of this writing.

Manufacturers on the Fence

Hyundai and Kia

Korean manufacturer Hyundai and its affiliate, Kia, had planned to begin selling a hybrid version of its compact Accent in Korea sometime in 2007, but announced in May 2006 that the introduction will be delayed until 2009.

Miles Johnson, a spokesman for Hyundai, said the hybrid car had not been slated for sale in the United States. "We're studying what would work best in the U.S.," he reported. "Yes, we know how to build hybrids but there is a lot of fluctuation in the U.S. market. Diesel technology is another application that we could do . . . We have an egg in every basket and we're waiting to see what shakes out."

Subaru

Subaru of America presented a powerful, hybrid-powered concept car at American auto shows in 2006, but it has announced that it will first concentrate on diesel engine development, with the goal of bringing out diesel cars by the end of 2007.

Toyota took an 8.7% stake in Fuji Heavy Industries, Subaru's parent company, in 2005. "Now that we are working with Toyota," said Dominic Infante, Subaru public relations manager, "we'll see what [hybrid technology] of theirs we can use and how it can work in our vehicles."

Mini USA

Jim McDowell, vice president of Mini USA, an independent brand of BMW, said, "We would love to have a hybrid Mini, but we have nothing to announce now." He added that there are no hybrids planned for the company's diminutive cars in 2006 or 2007.

The Plug-in Solution

Wouldn't it be great if you could hop in your automobile each morning and make the 30-mile round-trip to work and back without using so much as an ounce of gasoline or belching even a wisp of pollution into the air?

And wouldn't it be even more of a hoot if you could take that same car on weekend trips and vacations getting the same range and miles per gallon as conventional gasoline-electric hybrid vehicles—far less than the fuel required by gasoline-only cars?

Actually, this is not the stuff of dreams. It's a reality known as the *plug-in hybrid-electric vehicle*, or PHEV for short. There are only a few such automobiles on the road now, but that could change if the attention and support these new vehicles are gaining continues to grow.

How Plug-in Hybrids Work

The concept is not hard to understand. Take a gas-electric hybrid vehicle such as the Toyota Prius, upgrade its battery capacity, rig it so the vehicle will run for extended periods on electricity alone, and add a charger that can be plugged into the wall socket at home.

In essence, you have the best of two worlds: an all-electric vehicle for short trips and a gas-electric hybrid for more extensive driving. The combination could deliver an average 100 miles per gallon of gasoline.

"It's practical now," insists Felix Kramer, founder and lead spokesman for the California Cars Initiative, a group devoted to promoting fuel-efficient, nonpolluting automotive technologies.

Not everybody agrees. Despite enthusiasm from some very-high-profile people—President Bush included—general adoption of the technology in the near future is far from certain. There has been skepticism from automobile manufacturers, notably Toyota, and some people believe that plug-in costs, added to the estimated $3,000 premium for today's hybrid powertrains, may be more than the average consumer will accept.

Dave Hermance, Toyota executive engineer for advanced automotive technologies, agrees that plug-ins "are a good concept but, given today's battery technology, not yet."

The plug-in hybrid vehicle's control and display unit is mounted in front of the driver on this converted Toyota Prius.

The lithium-ion battery pack is stowed in the rear of a Toyota Prius that has been converted to a plug-in hybrid vehicle.

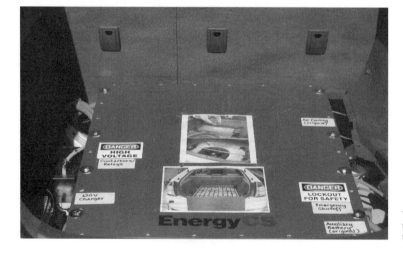

The cover warns everyone to be careful around the high-voltage lithium-ion battery pack in this Toyota Prius plug-in hybrid vehicle.

Passing motorists can't help but notice how fuel-efficient this Toyota Prius plug-in hybrid vehicle is.

He conceded that his concerns reflect the perspective of a major manufacturer that could face potentially huge liability claims if the batteries were not proven to be reliable and safe.

Nevertheless, Jim Press, Toyota of North America president, disclosed in July of 2006 that the company is pursuing a plug-in hybrid for the United States market. He did not discuss a production date.

Toyota's Prius has been the most popular car for plug-in conversion kits, but Toyota has announced that conversions will void the vehicle's warranties.

Kramer now drives along northern California roads in a Toyota Prius with a next-generation lithium-ion battery pack and a plug-in charger. In one five-day period he drove 195 miles at an average of 103 miles per gallon. Half of his driving was at highway speeds.

Equivalent-capacity lithium batteries weigh half as much as the nickel-metal hydride batteries used in today's mass-production hybrids. Kramer says that, with lithium-ion batteries, it's possible to make good PHEVs today—and even better ones in the coming years as their costs decline and performance and lifetime improve.

CalCars, as Kramer's group is called, says plug-in technology is "like having a second small fuel tank that you always use first. You get to fill this one at home with electricity at an equivalent cost of under $1 a gallon. How much under depends on your car and your electricity rate. You refill from an ordinary 120-volt socket, with energy that's much cleaner, cheaper, and not imported."

It also asserts that, "When gasoline costs three dollars a gallon, driving most gasoline cars costs eight to twenty cents a mile. With a plug-in hybrid, your local travel and commuting can go down to two to four cents a mile."

Although he has not put a lot of miles on his vehicle, Kramer scoffs at detractors who believe that the repeated charging and discharging of a PHEV's battery make today's nickel-metal hybride and lithium-ion batteries unacceptable for PHEVs. He points to Toyota's RAV4 E, the electric version of its popular compact SUV, which had nickel-metal hydride batteries that were more primitive than the NiMH batteries used in today's hybrids. "The batteries in those cars were supposed to last 75,000 miles. Some of those vehicles are still running very well at 125,000 miles," he said

Responding to the commonly held belief that fueling from the national power grid is "dirtier" than using gasoline, he claims that "well-to-wheel" greenhouse gases—the carbon dioxide resulting from all stages of producing, transporting, and using the electricity for plug-in cars—are less than half of what is generated by internal-combustion-engine cars.

Plug-ins on the Road

As of mid-2006, only one manufacturer had put plug-in hybrids on the road. DaimlerChrysler has a test fleet of specially converted Dodge Sprinter vans sprinkled across the United States, some using V-6 gasoline engines and some using five-cylinder diesel engines. The battery packs are nickel-metal hydride and lithium-ion.

Two companies plan to offer conversion kits. EDrive Systems, LLC, a southern California company, was expected to have one available in late 2006 for the Toyota Prius priced at $10,000 to $12,000. The firm's fourth prototype vehicle is the one being used by Kramer.

Hymotion, a Canadian firm, will have kits for the Prius, Ford Escape Hybrid, and Mercury Mariner available initially only for government and fleet orders. A consumer kit should be available in 2007. Prices are expected to start at $9,500.

Kramer sees those costs dropping as PHEVs gain acceptance and are mass- produced. "And," he points out, "if seventy-five percent of your driving is on electricity alone, that three-dollar-a-gallon gasoline averages out to about one dollar a gallon—maybe even fifty cents where electricity is cheap."

Meanwhile, if you're driving through northern California, you'll know for sure if you've crossed paths with one satisfied motorist. Kramer's white Prius announces to all in bold green letters "100+ MPG."

Although hybrid power is being developed in different ways by different manufacturers, all of the systems have one weakness in common: the battery pack. Nickel-metal hydride batteries are the electrical storage devices of choice in most hybrid vehicles now, and they represent a major advance over the traditional lead-acid batteries. But they are far from perfect.

What the manufacturers want, obviously, is a form of electrical storage that is smaller, lighter, and powerful enough to operate an electric motor that can propel a car or light truck by itself for extended periods. They would like one more thing, too: batteries that can be recharged quickly.

The next step most likely will be lithium-ion batteries, which are now used successfully to power cell phones and laptop computers. In a hybrid vehicle, these batteries would be more compact and two to three times as powerful as nickel-metal hydride batteries. But, they have not yet proven to be reliable or safe enough for automotive use. Widespread acceptance could be several years away.

Nevertheless, Subaru's parent, Fuji Heavy Industries, working with NEC Lamilion Energy, claims to have developed a manganese-lithium-ion battery that will last more than ten years and can charge in about five minutes.

Meanwhile, other researchers are concentrating on nickel batteries and even the traditional lead-acid batteries. Research is also progressing on another electrical storage device, the ultracapacitor, for vehicle use. Ultracapacitors can capture large amounts of electricity quickly during regenerative braking and release it quickly during acceleration.

The optimum device has not yet been perfected. But battery improvement is essential for the future of hybrid vehicles and the scientists are working hard to make it happen. The developer of the right electrical storage device will reap a huge payoff.

Alternative Fuels

Today's hybrid vehicles, and possibly tomorrow's plug-in hybrids, may provide a good way for the automotive industry to clean up exhaust emissions and lessen dependence on petroleum products. But a final solution, however far down the road, would be to develop a renewable fuel that would replace fossil fuels as a power source. Right now, there are two possibilities that show promise for at least reducing dependence on oil. One is ethanol—ethyl alcohol that is produced in the United States almost exclusively from corn, although it could be made from wheat, barley, and other plants and waste products. The second is biodiesel, a substitute for petroleum-based diesel fuel that can be formulated from fatty substances such as soybean oil and vegetable oil. Both are in production and in use on a limited basis in the United States. Each has attractive possibilities and some distinct disadvantages. Let's take a look at what role they might play in our automotive future.

Ethanol

Ethanol is now used exclusively as an additive to gasoline, although engines could be made to run on 100% ethanol. The most common blend is known as E10 because it contains 10% ethanol. One out of eight gallons of fuel sold in the United States is E10. It is compatible with all new vehicles sold in the United States over the last ten years and delivers nearly the same miles per gallon as straight gasoline. An oxygenate, it helps fuel to burn more cleanly and completely. It is replacing the chemical known as MTBE, another oxygenate that has been found to contaminate groundwater.

The other common blend is E85, which contains only 15% gasoline. In order to make a vehicle E85-compatible, vehicles must be equipped with a sensor that determines the amount of ethanol in the fuel. The sensor then recalibrates the engine. In addition, because ethanol is more corrosive than gasoline, the gas line, gas tanks, pumps, and fuel injectors must be modified. This costs an estimated $100 or more per vehicle. Ford, General Motors, and DaimlerChrysler have already produced nearly five million of these flex-fuel vehicles. General Motors is the biggest and most vocal backer of ethanol as an automotive fuel. The company promotes ethanol use in its multi-media advertising campaign, "Live Green, Go Yellow." General Motors has modified cars, sport-utility vehicles, and pickup trucks. Ford has flex-fuel capability in several sedans and one pickup truck. DaimlerChrysler has installed flex-fuel equipment in sedans, minivans, sport-utility vehicles, and pickup trucks.

Meanwhile, Jim Press, Toyota of North America president, disclosed in July of 2006 that Toyota may soon introduce flex-fuel vehicles in the United States.

To promote ethanol use, all race cars in the 2007 Indianapolis 500 will run on 100% ethanol.

⚙ **Advantages:** Ethanol burns cleaner than gasoline, is completely renewable, has the potential to cut down on oil imports, and has a favorable impact on the U.S. balance of payments because it is domestically produced. It also creates an expanded market for corn, potentially cutting down on the need for subsidies to farmers.

⚙ **Disadvantages:** At mid-year 2006, it was only available at about 700 service stations, mostly in the Midwest where corn is grown in abundance. Even with a 51-cent-a-gallon tax credit, E85 costs as much or more than gasoline in many areas. Although it is about 5% more powerful, it has less energy so the tank must be filled more often. A report from the Web site www.cars.com noted that a flex-fuel Chevrolet Impala with a 3.5-liter V-6 engine gets an EPA-rated 23 to 31 miles per gallon of gasoline and 16 to 23 miles per gallon of E85. The bottom line is that a gallon of E85 would have to cost 28% less than a gallon of gasoline for a motorist to break even.

Another complication is that ethanol cannot be delivered to distribution terminals through conventional pipelines because it gets pulled into the water that usually exists in conventional pipelines and tanks. Therefore, it must be trucked to terminals near the stations that sell it. Often, it is blended into gasoline right in the trucks that deliver it to the stations.

Studies also vary on how much conventional energy is required to produce the ethanol. One study, conducted at Cornell University, claims that production of ethanol consumes 29% more energy than it yields. The American Institute of Biological Services says ethanol yields 10% more energy than it takes to produce it. Numerous other studies, however, have concluded that ethanol yields a third or more energy than it takes to produce it.

Why Manufacturers Love E85

In mid-2006, General Motors, Ford, and Chrysler were boasting that each had built more than 1.5 million vehicles capable of running on pure gasoline or E85 and that many more were on the way.

The conversion is not free. It costs the manufacturers an estimated $100 or more per vehicle, or an approximate total expenditure of about $500 million. Yet, the flex-fuel option is given to the buyer for free.

At the same time, there were only about 700 service stations, mostly in the Midwest, capable of delivering E85 to the millions of flex-fuel vehicles.

What's going on here?

For the answer, turn to the government's Corporate Average Fuel Economy (CAFE) regulations. Right now, the manufacturers must maintain an average fuel efficiency of 27.5 miles per gallon for cars and 22.5 miles per gallon for light trucks. There are substantial fines for missing these mandates.

In order to stimulate the use of alternative fuels, however, the government credits flexible-fuel vehicles with delivering better mileage than they actually do. The fiction can boost the overall fuel efficiency of a manufacturer's fleet by as much as .9 miles per gallon.

In effect, the more flex-fuel vehicles a manufacturer sells, the more gas guzzlers it can produce without failing to meet the mandated averages.

It doesn't matter that ethanol is less efficient than gasoline or that buyers may never put a gallon of E85 in their cars. It saves the companies penalties that are much more substantial than $100 per vehicle.

Finally, according to the American Coalition for Ethanol, in 2005 it took 14% (1.6 billion bushels) of the total U.S. corn crop (11.1 billion bushels) to produce 3% (4 billion gallons) of the total annual gasoline consumption (140 billion gallons). Even with a major expansion of corn growing, corn-based ethanol can never fill all the energy needs of vehicles in the United States.

Still, ethanol is not being written off as a viable substitute for gasoline. Producers are exploring methods to produce *cellulosic ethanol*, which is chemically identical to corn-based ethanol. Cellulose, the most common organic compound on earth, is the main component of plant cell walls and is found in abundance in many materials regarded as unusable: grass, wood chips, straw, switchgrass, even municipal waste. If a technique can be perfected to produce ethanol economically from cellulose, it would greatly increase the volume of ethanol that could be produced. A joint study of the U.S. Department of Energy and the U.S. Department of Agriculture projected that it may be possible to produce enough cellulosic ethanol to displace 30% of the country's oil use. The Department of Energy also has estimated that perfection of production techniques could reduce the cost of a gallon of ethanol by sixty cents in the year 2015. Several companies, most notably the Canadian biotechnology firm Iogen, were working to produce cellulosic ethanol in mid-2006.

Biodiesel

Another alternative source of fuel, biodiesel can be made from vegetable oils, recycled grease, or animal fat. However, commercially sold fuel-grade biodiesel must meet industry standards to assure proper performance and requirements of the 1990 Clean Air Act amendments. Raw vegetable oil cannot meet biodiesel fuel specifications, it is not registered with the EPA, and it is not a legal motor fuel. Nevertheless, biodiesel can be made from waste grease and used cooking oils. The Internet contains several recipes for diesel-vehicle owners to make the fuel at home. Perhaps the most famous proponent of biodiesel is country-western singer Willie Nelson. He's part of a company that markets BioWillie biodiesel to truck stops.

Blended with regular diesel fuel as B2 (2% biodiesel) or B5 (5% biodiesel), it can be used in most diesel-engine cars and trucks without modification. Some engines can be modified to use B20 and even B100. It is made by chemically reacting oil or fat with alcohol. The major products are the fuel and glycerol, which is used to make soap and cosmetic products. In the United States (the second largest producer), biodiesel is generally made from soybean oil. In Europe (the No. 1 consumer of biodiesel), it's generally made from rapeseed oil. Biodiesel production in 2005 tripled over the year before, to an estimated 75 million gallons, and the growth was expected to continue with the construction of numerous new production plants.

With tougher standards for diesel fuel now going into effect in the United States, it appears that more manufacturers will be offering diesel-powered vehicles for sale. That could be the catalyst to find less expensive ways to produce biodiesel and to open the door for even greater production and availability.

⚙ **Advantages:** It is completely renewable, it pollutes less than petroleum, it has the potential to reduce dependence on foreign oil, it is a better lubricant than regular diesel fuel, it contributes to longer engine life, it has no sulfur so it can extend the life of catalytic converters, it yields three times the energy needed to produce it, and it returns essentially the same fuel mileage.

⚙ **Disadvantages:** When produced from soybeans, which are only 20% oil, it is significantly more expensive than petroleum-based diesel fuel. It can damage rubber hoses in older vehicles. It cleans dirt from engines, which then clogs filters. It tends to gel at temperatures slightly above freezing. It is not conveniently available across the United States, particularly in the West.

Hydrogen

Hydrogen probably won't be a fuel of convenience anytime soon, but it's easy to understand why manufacturers are concentrating so much effort into developing it for automotive applications. Hydrogen is the most common element and is nonpolluting.

Many manufacturers have developed fuel cells, containers in which hydrogen interacts with oxygen to form water and in the process produces electricity. That electricity is directed to an electric motor that powers the car. There is no need to generate electricity for storage in batteries, as is the case with hybrids, because the fuel cells can supply continuous power as long as there is a constant supply of hydrogen and oxygen.

The hydrogen gas is fed into fuel tanks just as gasoline is and then sent to the fuel cell. However, because the gas has very low density, it must be stored under high pressure so that enough energy will be captured to give the vehicle an acceptable range before needing a refill. Tanks already in use in developmental vehicles such as the Honda FCX hold hydrogen gas compressed to 5,000 pounds of pressure per square inch, and that allows a traveling range of about 200 miles.

At the bottom line, what fuel cells make possible is propulsion by a nonpolluting electric motor, something the auto industry has been trying without much success to accomplish for more than a century with battery power.

Several other manufacturers, most notably BMW, are working on another approach. They use liquefied hydrogen as a fuel to power an internal combustion engine much the same way that gasoline does. A few such pollution-free vehicles are being developed and tested right now but, as is the case with fuel-cell vehicles, obstacles remain before they can join the mainstream. To turn hydrogen into a liquid, for example, it must be reduced to -441°F. A BMW fuel tank has been developed that can maintain the liquid state when the car is in use. However, if it is parked for an extended period of time, the surrounding warmth will cause the hydrogen to expand and some will escape as gas.

Nevertheless, BMW has announced that production of a hydrogen-fueled 7 Series sedan will begin by 2008. The car will have two fuel tanks, one for hydrogen and the other for gasoline. The German manufacturer has chosen the flagship sedan because it is its only model large enough to accommodate two separate fuel tanks. The company did not say where the twin-fuel car would be sold.

A huge challenge for both forms of hydrogen power is the creation of a fueling infrastructure to conveniently accommodate hydrogen-powered vehicles. It

Top: Honda's next generation hydrogen-powered car will look very much like this prototype.

Bottom: The hydrogen-powered 2006 Honda FCX has been driven in the Los Angeles area for more than a year by one California family.

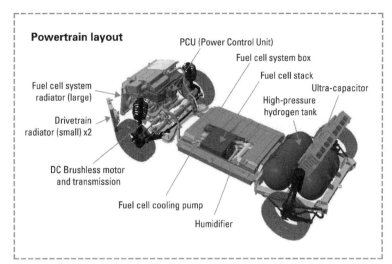

Powertrain layout

PCU (Power Control Unit)

Fuel cell system box

Fuel cell stack

Fuel cell system radiator (large)

Ultra-capacitor

High-pressure hydrogen tank

Drivetrain radiator (small) x2

DC Brushless motor and transmission

Fuel cell cooling pump

Humidifier

The Honda FCX – minus its body.

has been estimated that it would cost $450,000 to add low-volume hydrogen refueling to a gas station. There are approximately 180,000 gas stations in the United States.

Unlike oxygen, which exists in air, hydrogen is generally part of another compound, so it must be chemically decoupled. The predominant method used in the automotive industry is to extract it from natural gas, but it could be obtained from coal, gasoline, methanol, and even ethanol. Because a fuel cell powering an electric motor is two to three times as efficient as an internal combustion engine, fossil-fuel-based hydrogen power may prove to be a long-term way of reducing dependence on oil. But, like gasoline itself, it is not a final solution. To truly move away from nonrenewable, petroleum-based fuels, hydrogen must be obtained by some other means. The obvious alternative, experts feel, is electrolysis, a process by which hydrogen and oxygen are separated from water. That requires a lot of electricity, which would have to come from solar energy, wind farms, hydroelectric plants, or, most efficiently, nuclear plants. Hydrogen power for automobiles may arrive within a decade or two, but total independence from fossil fuels is a long way off.

⚙ **Advantages:** It is an abundant element. It is nonpolluting. It's an efficient form of power. It could be extracted from water.

⚙ **Disadvantages:** As a gas or liquid, it must be stored under extremely high pressure. There is no delivery system. It is now derived mainly from natural gas, another nonrenewable fuel. Extracting hydrogen from water requires a lot of electricity.

Natural Gas

All but one manufacturer have moved away from natural gas as an alternative fuel, claiming that there has been little customer demand and that there is an insufficient network of fueling stations where natural gas can be obtained.

The lone holdout is Japanese manufacturer Honda, which is selling its Honda Civic GX to fleet operators, both private and public, that have their own fueling stations, and to select dealers in California and New York. To make the Civic GX more convenient to individual buyers, it also is offering a home refilling station that can tap into the fuel lines of owners who heat their homes with natural gas. Natural gas is approximately one-third to one-half cheaper than an equivalent amount of gasoline.

Based on the 2006 Civic, the GX has a four-cylinder powerplant that has been rated the "cleanest internal combustion engine on Earth" by the U.S. Environmental Protection Agency. The 1.8-liter powerplant produces 113 horsepower and 109 foot-pounds of torque. The GX, equipped standard with a full complement of safety features, air-conditioning, stereophonic sound system, and a five-speed automatic transmission, gets an EPA-rated 28 miles per gallon of gas in the city and 39 on the highway. It has a range of about 200 miles.

Honda sells the car for $24,990, but owners qualify for a federal tax credit of $4,000. The home refueling device, known as Phill, can be mounted to a garage wall or outdoors and retails for about $3,500, plus $1,000 or more for installation.

A small badge tells the world which Honda Civics are powered by natural gas.

It is eligible for a $1,000 tax credit. Owners who don't want to buy the device can lease one from Honda.

✪ **Advantages:** Natural gas is clean burning and cheaper than gasoline.

✪ **Disadvantages:** Honda is the only producer of natural gas automobiles and it sells them only in select areas of California and New York. It is only available at an extremely limited number of filling stations. Home refilling stations are expensive.

A home filling station, below, can be used to fill the tank of Honda's natural-gas powered Civic, below left.

A Cheaper Jet Fuel?

Alternative fuels may make good sense for cars and trucks, even boats and trains—but jet planes?

Yes, maybe even jet planes. The *New York Times* has reported that the U.S. Air Force is conducting tests to see if jets can fly safely on a blend of traditional jet fuel and a synthetic liquid made from natural gas. The synthetic fuel could eventually be made from coal, which is much cheaper and more plentiful.

According to the *Times,* the Air Force consumed 3.2 billion gallons of aviation fuel in fiscal 2005, slightly more than half of all petroleum used by the federal government. A single F-16 fighter jet can consume 28 gallons of fuel a minute.

The Air Force fuel bill for the year was $4.7 billion. Still, the entire government's share of national fuel usage is only 1.7%.

Electricity

Contrary to what many believe, it is possible to obtain a vehicle that operates strictly on electricity. In fact, you can get electric bicycles, electric scooters, electric golf carts, electric commuter cars, electric performance cars, and even electric-powered replicas of classic antique cars.

Most are sold by niche marketers, but Global Motor Cars, a division of DaimlerChrysler, offers a line of five golf-cart-like vehicles that can carry from two to six passengers. Two models have beds for hauling. They will go 25 miles per hour and have a range of 30 to 50 miles, depending on the load and road conditions. They are street legal on low-speed roads in some states. Prices range from $7,000 to $12,500.

Commuter Cars Corporation, a Spokane, Washington, company, has built the Tango, an electric super car that movie star George Clooney owns. Company President Rick Woodbury says it can travel from a stop to 60 miles an hour in 4 seconds, reach a top speed of 150 mph, and go about 60 miles on the power supplied by its lead-acid batteries. The company is building Tango 600s for two more customers, and those vehicles will have more modern nickel-metal hydride batteries that will extend the range to between 100 and 120 miles. The Tango is narrower than some motorcycles, but as stable as a sports car. It holds a driver and one passenger or cargo behind the driver. It has a carbon-fiber body shell and a race-approved roll-cage structure, making it safe for use in all traffic conditions. Inside, it has leather seats, climate control, and a premium audio

Electricity alone can move the motorcycle-sized Tango from a stop to 60 miles an hour in 4 seconds.

Future Hybrids and Alternative-Fuel Vehicles

Actor George Clooney owns and drives a $108,000 Tango 600 electric car.

system. The super car's super price is $108,000. Tango also plans to build a Tango 200 and Tango 100, less-powerful, less-expensive electric cars that will be available about two years after the company receives necessary funding.

⚙ **Advantages:** Electricity is nonpolluting and available almost anywhere.

⚙ **Disadvantages:** Electric vehicles have extremely short range. Recharging batteries is time-consuming and makes long-distance driving impractical.

Fuel-Sipping Minicars

With the exception of the Volkswagen Beetle, U.S. motorists didn't think much of small, inexpensive, fuel-sipping cars until the 1970s. But, the idea that econocars could be desirable forms of transportation took root quickly as the country suffered through its first gas crisis with alternate-day availability and long lines at the pumps. Unfortunately, U.S. manufacturers, long accustomed to the bigger-is-better mentality of American car buyers, didn't have any small cars to sell back then and deluded themselves into thinking that they would never really catch on.

The gates were wide open, and in rushed Toyota, Honda, Nissan (known as Datsun at the time), Subaru, Volkswagen Audi, and others with their small, efficient, capable cars. The United States eventually got into the compact market, but by then most of the foreign manufacturers had secured a place in the United States market that for most has continued to grow until this day.

Their cars have grown, too. The 2006 Honda Civic, for example, seems almost like a full-size sedan compared to the tiny car that putt-putted its way into the United States in 1972. Similar growth spurts have afflicted many of the compact cars.

With hybrid vehicles commanding a premium price, and alternative-fuel cars not widely available, many manufacturers are going back to what worked before: small, affordable cars with conventional engines that are extremely fuel efficient. This time the U.S. manufacturers have a supply of their own compact cars, but, as before, the foreigners can undersize them because they have been manufacturing the subcompacts for use in other countries.

Here, in alphabetical order, are the newest small cars that were being sold in the United States in mid-2006.

Chevrolet Aveo
EPA Ratings: 24–35 mpg

Actually produced by Daewoo, a Korean subsidiary of General Motors, the Chevrolet Aveo four-door sedan and four-door hatchback models have been redesigned for 2007. Slightly larger, with room for four adults and 12.3 cubic feet of luggage space, the front-wheel-drive Aveos come in three trim levels.

The Special Value edition starts at $9,890, the LS starts at $11,900, and the LT starts at $13,590. All have the same 1.6-liter, 103-horsepower, four-cylinder engine. The Special Value edition comes only with a five-speed manual transmission. The other models offer the choice of a four-speed automatic or a five-speed manual. Standard transmission models are EPA-rated at 26 miles per gallon in the city and 35 on the highway. Automatic Aveos are rated at 24 mpg city/34 mpg highway. The sedan will hold 11.6 cubic feet of luggage; the hatchback will hold 7.1 cubic feet with seatbacks up, 42 cubic feet with rear seatbacks folded.

The Chevrolet Aveo is a small but roomy subcompact sedan.

Dodge Caliber

EPA Ratings: 23–32 mpg

The biggest among the new small automobiles, the Dodge Caliber—a macho-looking, SUV-like four-door hatchback that holds up to five passengers—replaces the aging Neon. It comes in three trim lines, has three available engines, two transmissions, and the choice of front- or all-wheel drive. DaimlerChrysler built it as a world car and hopes to sell it in 100 countries.

For the United States, the front-wheel-drive SE model is the least expensive, with a base price of $13,985. It comes with a standard 1.8-liter, 148-horsepower, four-cylinder engine and a five-speed manual transmission. The U.S. Environmental Protection Agency estimates fuel efficiency at 28 miles per gallon in the city and 32 mpg on the highway. A 2-liter, 158-horsepower, four-cylinder engine (26 mpg city/30 mpg highway) is optional. A continuously variable automatic transmission is available with either engine. The front-wheel-drive Caliber SXT, with a base price of $15,985, has the same engine and transmission choices but more standard features.

The top-of-the-line, all-wheel-drive Caliber R/T, starting at $19,985, is the most powerful, with a 2.4-liter, 172-horsepower, four-cylinder engine. The only transmission choice is the continuously variable automatic. The EPA estimates fuel mileage at 23 mpg in the city, 26 mpg on the highway.

The Caliber's cargo capacity is rated at 18.5 cubic feet with the rear seatbacks up and 48 cubic feet with the seats folded flat.

DaimlerChrysler will also offer the Caliber with a 2-liter turbodiesel engine supplied by Volkswagen. It will be the most fuel-efficient powerplant, but the manufacturer said at the car's introduction that it has no plans to make the diesel available in the United States.

The Dodge Caliber hatchback opens to a maximum 48 cubic feet of cargo space.

The Dodge Caliber is a completely different vehicle than the Neon it replaces.

Fuel-Sipping Minicars

Honda Fit

EPA Ratings: 31–38 mpg

The Japanese manufacturer that made its name in the United States with well-made, well-equipped small cars returns to its roots with the Fit, a front-wheel-drive, four-door hatchback that is tiny on the outside, surprisingly big on the inside, and relatively inexpensive.

A mere 157.4 inches in length, it is 20 inches shorter and 3 inches narrower than a Honda Civic sedan. Yet, it can swallow 21.3 cubic feet of cargo with its rear seatbacks in place and nearly 42 cubic feet of stuff when its 60/40 rear seatback is folded flat. Compare that to the Civic's 12-cubic-foot cargo capacity. There are two main reasons for the Fit's clever packaging. It is 4 inches taller than a Civic, and its gas tank is located under the front seat to allow a lower rear floor.

The 1.5-liter, 109-horsepower, four-cylinder engine, teamed up with a five-speed manual transmission, can return an EPA-calculated average of 33 mpg city/38 mpg highway. Equipped with an optional five-speed automatic transmission, the Fit's fuel mileage drops a bit to an estimated 31 mpg city/38 mpg highway.

Base price is $13,850. Although new to the United States, the Fit is available in more than seventy countries and more than one million have been sold. The vehicle is called the Jazz in Europe.

Inside, the tiny Honda Fit is surprisingly roomy for up to four people. It may be short, but the Honda Fit stands tall.

Hyundai Accent

EPA Ratings: 28–37 mpg

The third-generation Hyundai Accent comes in three- and four-door models and offers something that the other small cars do not: a five-year, 60,000-mile bumper-to-bumper warranty.

The three-door GS and SE models went on sale during the spring of 2006 as 2007 models. The top-of-the-line four-door GLS went on sale several months earlier as a 2006 model. Base prices range from $10,415 for a base GS model with five-speed manual transmission to $14,915 for a sport-oriented Accent SE three-door with a four-speed automatic transmission.

Powering all three models is a 1.6-liter, 110-horsepower, four-cylinder engine that can be mated with a five-speed manual transmission or a four-speed automatic shifter. The manual transmission models are rated at 32 mpg city/35 mpg highway and the automatics at 28 mpg city/37 mpg highway. All of the Korean-made Accents have room for four adults. The three-door model has 15.9 cubic feet of luggage space. The four-door sedan has 12.4 cubic feet of luggage space.

The Hyundai Accent is available as a four-door sedan or as a three-door hatchback.

Kia Rio

EPA Ratings: 28–36 mpg

A corporate cousin to the Hyundai Accent, the front-wheel-drive Kia Rio is offered as a sedan with two trim levels, and as a four-door hatchback called the Kia Rio5. All three models come with the same engine and transmission options as the Accent, the same basic warranty, and nearly identical fuel efficiency ratings.

The four-passenger sedans are very close in all dimensions to the Accent. The Rio5 is about 10 inches shorter but offers better cargo space because of its hatchback configuration. The sedan trunk will hold 11.9 cubic feet of luggage. The Rio5 can hold 15.8 cubic feet of cargo with the rear seatback up, and 49.6 cubic feet with the seatback folded down.

The base Rio sedan starts at $11,310, LX pricing begins at $13,185, and the Rio5 starts at $14,240.

The Kia Rio features a 110-horsepower engine and either a five-speed manual or four-speed automatic transmission.

Nissan Versa

EPA Ratings: 28–36 mpg

The Nissan Versa, known as the Tiida elsewhere in the world, is on sale in the United States as a front-wheel-drive, four-door hatchback. A sedan version will be added in early 2007.

There are two trim levels, S and SL. In the S model, with a base price of $13,055, the 1.8-liter, 122-horsepower, four-cylinder engine is mated to either a six-speed manual or a four-speed automatic transmission. The SL model, starting at $15,055, can be purchased with the same engine mated to either a six-speed manual or a continuously variable transmission. Manual transmission models are rated by the U.S. Environmental Protection Agency at 30 mpg city-34 mpg highway, four-speed automatics at 28/35, and continuously variable automatics at 30/36. Cargo space is 18 cubic feet with the rear seatback up and 50 cubic feet with it folded down. The back seat is large enough to hold three adults — at least on short trips.

The Nissan Versa four-door hatchback, available in 2006, will be joined by a Versa sedan in early 2007.

Suzuki Reno

EPA Ratings: 22–30 mpg

Another car made by Korean manufacturer Daewoo, the front-wheel-drive Suzuki Reno comes with a 2-liter, 126-horsepower, four-cylinder engine and either a five-speed manual or four-speed automatic transmission.

There are three trim levels: the S starts at $13,499, the LX starts at $15,349, and the EX starts at $17,049. The automatic transmission is optional on the S and LX models, standard on the EX. Fuel mileage with both transmissions is rated at 22 mpg city/30 mpg highway. The four-door hatchback is big enough to hold up to five passengers. Cargo space is 9 cubic feet with the rear seatback up, 45 cubic feet with it folded down.

The Suzuki Reno, manufactured in Korea, can hold up to five people or 45 cubic feet of cargo.

Toyota Yaris

EPA Ratings: 34–40 mpg

The Toyota Yaris is a new name only in the United States. The replacement for the basically unloved Toyota Echo has been on the road for years in Europe and Japan and has been honored as Car of the Year in both places.

Two distinct front-wheel-drive models are being sold in the United States: a three-door hatchback that was designed in Europe and a four-door sedan that was designed in Japan. They are different in appearance and detail, but both are propelled by a 1.5-liter, 106-horsepower, four-cylinder engine and either a five-speed manual or four-speed automatic transmission. Manual transmission models get an estimated 34 mpg city/40 mpg highway, and the automatics get an estimated 34 mpg city/39 mpg highway.

Cargo space in the hatchback model is 9.3 cubic feet with the rear seatback up, 25.7 with it down. The sedan's trunk has 12.9 cubic feet and can be expanded to 13.7 cubic feet with the rear seatback down.

The two-door hatchback has a starting price of $10,950, the sedan starts at $11,825, and the S sedan starts at $13,325.

An award winner in Europe and Japan, the Toyota Yaris is now available in the United States as a four-door sedan or a three-door hatchback.

There are a few cars on the road today that can rocket from a stop to 60 miles per hour in less than five seconds. And there are others that can average 50 miles per gallon of fuel. Wouldn't it be great if you could find one that could do both?

Actually, you can. But don't look to Detroit, or Germany, or Japan, or any place else where cars are normally built.

Instead, take a ride to West Philadelphia High School in Pennsylvania and look up Simon Hauger and his 10th through 12th grade students at the Academy for Automotive and Mechanical Engineering. They can show you how to put together a super two-seater than can run with the fastest and the most frugal cars on the planet. And, as an added bonus, they'll tell you how the car can run more than 50 miles on a gallon of nonpolluting soybean oil. No soybeans? No problem. You can get the same performance on regular diesel fuel.

The secret to achieving the best of both worlds is hybrid power. In this case, Hauger and his students mated a diesel engine with a powerful electric motor. The electric motor turns the front wheels and the diesel engine supplies power to the rear.

The two-seat super sports car is the result of a class project begun several years ago. It has been evolving ever since and it has brought teacher and students numerous accolades.

"It's all off-the-shelf technology," Hauger explained. "We're not 180 IQ people around here." The idea for the car was developed in the 2002-2003 school year. Construction was begun the next year and the car was finished during the 2004–2005 year.

Hauger, a physics teacher, put the project cost at about $25,000, but emphasized that the real costs were greatly offset by contributions from businesses and individuals. "We've estimated that there is probably between $80,000 and $100,000 worth of parts in the car," he said.

Teacher and students began with a 1.9-liter, 90-horsepower turbodiesel engine and a five-speed manual transmission extracted from a Volkswagen. A kit-car frame called the Attack, manufactured by K-1 Engineering, had to be modified to make room for the engine, motor, suspension, cooling system, and related parts. That's because it was originally designed to accommodate the mechanical components of a Honda Accord.

Carbon-fiber body panels were donated by Hexcel Corp. of Stamford, Connecticut, and the wheels and tires were donated by OZ Racing. Sun Oil Co. donated $5,000. The finished car weighs about 2,200 pounds.

During the next two years, they built their sports car, installed the diesel drivetrain, and set the whole thing up to work in conjunction with a 200-horsepower electric motor. Tests conducted in the shop indicated that the car would be capable of running from a stop to 60 mph in less than four seconds. Then, trouble cropped up with the battery pack, so teacher and students moved to plan B. They dismantled the hybrid electronics, installed synthetic rubber fuel lines to accommodate the soybean extract, and entered the sports car in the 2005 Tour de Sol, an annual event held to spot-

The hybrid hot rod built by West Philadelphia (Pa.) High School students has been a Tour de Sol winner two years in a row.

light the possibilities of alternate energy sources for transportation. The car averaged 51 miles per gallon in the competition, and came in first in the alternative-fuel class.

The victory was especially sweet for everyone connected with the automotive academy. As a result of the first-place finish, the program was spared from proposed budget cutbacks and possible disbandment.

Hauger couldn't have been more pleased, because the automotive program is one of the success stories in an inner-city school where it is often hard to encourage students from impoverished families to get an education and finish school.

"Kids really get into it," Hauger said. "Some have gone to Drexel, some to Lincoln Technical, some to automotive training centers. One kid's doing real well. It won't be long until he's making more money than I am."

Unfortunately, the team was still without an acceptable source of electrical power as of 2006. So, it entered the 2006 Tour de Sol under biodiesel power again. The difference was an updated computer chip that raised horsepower to 150. They came in first in the Hybrid and Alternative-Fuels Division, winning the acceleration competition and the fuel efficiency leg with an average of 55 miles per gallon. Even without the aid of an electric motor, the car can now run from a stop to 60 miles per hour in a little over five seconds.

But Hauger and his students are moving ahead with hybrid power. They are now working with AC Propulsion to obtain a proper battery pack for their tiny roadster. Hauger is confident the hybrid road rocket will be able to hit 60 mph in less than four seconds and still return exceptional fuel mileage.

It sounds like 2007 will be another fast and furious year for the innovative and talented gang from West Philadelphia High School.

100 Miles Per Gallon: Is That All?

When you stop to think about it, maybe 50 or even 100 miles to a gallon of gasoline isn't all that great. Just a couple of years ago, when fuel was half the price it is today, a car that got 25 miles to a gallon could travel the same distance for the same price as today's 50 mpg car. Sure, you're stretching a gallon of fuel. But you haven't made your money go any farther. Can't we do better? Some people say, "Yes." How would you like . . .

250 Miles Per Gallon?

This may sound a bit extreme, but the folks at AFS Trinity Power Corporation, a Bellevue, Washington, company, are dead serious and say they have the technology to build a hybrid car capable of traveling more than 250 miles on a gallon of gasoline or ethanol. They've even filed an application for a patent.

Just like the plug-in hybrids being touted today, the car dubbed Extreme Hybrid would have to be plugged into the owner's house electricity current each night. But, the company says, its system incorporates technology "to overcome the limits of the energy storage components of conventional hybrids and other plug-in designs."

A five-passenger Extreme Hybrid would have performance comparable to today's vehicles and would be able to travel up to 40 miles on electric power alone. For longer trips, it would operate as a conventional hybrid.

AFS Trinity and Ricardo, a global automotive engineering firm, are working together to design, test, and develop the Extreme Hybrid drivetrain and build the systems that AFS Trinity would license to manufacturers worldwide.

Edward W. Furia, chairman and chief executive officer of AFS Trinity, reported at mid-year that, "The power electronics, ultracapacitors, batteries, motors, and other related components that we will integrate with Ricardo's help into the Extreme Hybrid drivetrain are all advancing rapidly and reducing in cost."

Furia noted that the average American driver goes about 300 miles a week and, at $3 a gallon, spends $45 if the car gets 20 miles per gallon, $36 if the vehicle gets 25 miles per gallon. "By comparison," he said, "the Extreme Hybrid will use less than $8 per week total for fuel and electricity."

"The Extreme Hybrid . . . will also be the first hybrid that will save enough money from reduced operating costs to more than offset the higher purchase price of the car," Furia added. No purchase price was disclosed, but he predicted an Extreme Hybrid owner would be ahead by $11,000 over five years.

The company says demonstration vehicles could be available to fleet owners in 2008 and mass production could begin in 2009.

That would be a good start, for sure, but how would you like . . .

330 Miles Per Gallon?

If there weren't already a movie by that name, Steve Fambro's decision to start his own car company and build a super-efficient hybrid car might well be called *Against All Odds*.

But he can be found, day after day, in an airplane hangar working on the Aptera, a bug-like, rear-wheel-drive, two-seat coupe he says will move from a stop to 60 miles per hour in 11 seconds, reach a top speed of 95 mph, weigh 850 pounds, meet all safety standards, travel 330 miles per gallon of fuel at 65 mph, and, oh yes, cost less than $20,000.

And how, exactly, does he expect to accomplish all that? The Carlsbad, California, electrical engineer says his small team will coordinate a clean-burning, 12-horsepower diesel engine with a 25-horsepower electric motor, transmit power through a continuously variable automatic transmission, and wrap it all up in what he calls *Panelized Automated Composite Construction*. The energy absorbing composite materials he is working with are already used in high-tech race cars and in aircraft. In fact, his car takes a lot of cues from airplanes. It will have only three wheels (two in front, one at the rear), and they will be shrouded to reduce wind resistance. Even the name is telling. Aptera comes from a Greek word meaning *flight without wings*.

Fambro's confidence notwithstanding, the experts say he has probably embarked on a project best described by another movie title, *Mission: Impossible*. Still, Fambro announced a deal with a Canadian composite company in early

No, it's not ET's car, it's the Aptera. Builder Steve Fambro's dream is for the Aptera to travel safely on U.S. roads, cost less than $20,000, and get unheard-of fuel mileage.

2006 and at mid-year reported that, "The project is going well and we have funding." He was hoping to have a car on the road by the end of 2006.

If his dream comes true, Aptera owners will be able to drive for a week on less than a gallon of fuel. That sounds great now, but there is always someone looking for more. How would you like . . .

10,000 Miles Per Gallon?

Actually, this is old news. A French team, Microjoule, set the world fuel economy record in 2003, averaging 10,705 miles per gallon during the Shell Eco-Marathon at the Rockingham Motor Speedway in England.

Yes, there is a catch. The competing teams were required only to travel 7 miles on the banked track at a speed that exceeded 15 miles an hour. The team of French engineering students put their unique vehicle in the hands of their smallest member, a 12-year-old boy, to keep the weight down.

The 7-mile journey was hardly a pleasure trip. The ground-hugging, aerodynamic three-wheeler had no windows and barely enough room for its diminutive pilot to be seated in a recumbent position. In his airless confines, he was required to steer and run the tiny gasoline engine just enough to maintain the required speed.

After the event, team manager Jean Charles Boulerie put his team's hard work into perspective. "It is a brilliant result for us," he said, "and shows we were right to persevere over the winter refining this incredible machine . . . but the challenge now is to construct a vehicle that can achieve this sort of result in day-to-day motoring at speeds somewhat in excess of fifteen miles per hour."

Maybe . . . and Finally

Those numbers are otherworldly now—and no doubt will remain so forever. Still, wouldn't it be great to fill the tank on the day you buy your car and never have to add gasoline again? Just about anybody would go for that.

It's hard to tell just where real-world technology will lead the automobile industry. But a couple of things appear certain at this time. Some form of personal transportation will probably be around forever, and fossil fuel will not. Maybe one of today's dreamers will be the architect of tomorrow's solution.

{Acknowledgments}

Writing about hybrid cars and alternative fuels has been a rewarding educational experience for me, and I am happy to say that I have had a lot of good teachers along the way.

First of all, I would like to thank Maureen Graney, editor-in-chief of The Lyons Press, who nursed an aging rookie through the organization and presentation of this book. Writing a book is a lot different than writing newspaper and magazine articles, and I doubt I could have accomplished the task without her guidance.

I would also like to thank Gene Brissie, Lyons associate publisher, for giving me the opportunity to expand my writing horizons with a book about automotive developments, a subject that is always close to my heart. In addition, I would like to express my appreciation to Jennifer Taber, assistant editor, for help in assembling the pictures for the hybrid book; Mark Keegan, art director; Georgiana Goodwin, book designer; Kevin Lynch, production director; and Nancy Freeborn, a Toyota Prius driver who executed the design.

In a career of newspapering, I have never found any public relations professionals to be more courteous and helpful than the men and women in the automotive business. Their patience, their willingness to find and supply information, their guidance, and their help in putting me in touch with industry professionals who could answer my many questions is not just appreciated, it was crucial.

Among the many who helped, I would like to make special mention of a few: Wade Hoyt, northeast region public relations manager for Toyota; Chris Naughton, East Coast regional public relations manager for Honda; and Octavio Navarro, product news manager in Ford's New York office. In addition, special thanks to Jon Lorensen's Westbrook Honda in Westbrook, Connecticut, for letting us photograph the engine of an Insight.

Finally, I would like to thank a few whose technical expertise was invaluable in helping me to explain the intricacies of hybrid vehicles and alternative fuels: Dave Hermance, Toyota's chief engineer for advanced technology vehicles; Felix Kramer, founder of the nonprofit California Cars Initiative; Brian Corbett, General Motors spokesman who guided me through the nuances of the two-mode hybrid; and Charles Ofria, who operates the popular Web site www.familycar.com and knows a lot about all things automotive.

If I owned a hat, it would be off to all of you.

{Useful Web Sites}

These Web sites are among many that offer a wealth of information to people who are interested in buying or simply learning about hybrid and alternative-fuel vehicles. The answers to specific questions about hybrids and alternative-fuel vehicles can usually be found by accessing a search site and typing in key words.

Hybrid Vehicle Manufacturers
www.ford.com
www.gm.com
www.honda.com
www.toyota.com

General Information on Hybrid and Alternative-Fuel Vehicles
www.aceee.org
The American Council for an Energy-Efficient Economy Web site provides information on federal and state tax incentives for hybrid and alternative-fuel vehicles.

www.calcars.org
The California Cars Initiative Web site provides information on plug-in hybrids.

www.eere.energy.gov/afdc
The U.S. Department of Energy's Web site for its Alternative Fuels Data Center provides information on alternative fuels, alternative-fuel vehicles, and locations where alternative fuels can be purchased.

www.fueleconomy.gov
The U.S. Department of Energy's official site for fuel-economy data, federal tax incentives, and information on hybrid cars and alternative fuels.

www.greencarcongress.com

Provides information on technology advances and other issues regarding hybrid vehicles.

www.greenercars.com

The ACEEE's Green Book ranks cars, trucks, minivans, and sport-utility vehicles according to their environmental friendliness.

www.greenhybrid.com

Offers information on hybrid cars and allows owners and other interested parties to exchange information.

www.howstuffworks.com

Offers an easy-to-follow explanation of how the various hybrid power-plants work.

www.hybridcars.com

Offers up-to-date information on hybrid cars, hybrid technology, fuel prices, the environment, and more.

www.hybridcenter.org

The Union of Concerned Scientists offers a variety of information on hybrid vehicles and an up-to-date list of federal and state tax incentives.

www.mixedpower.com

This Web site provides information by and for hybrid vehicle owners.

Useful Web Sites

{Photo Credits}

Page iii: Photo courtesy of Toyota

Page vii: Photo courtesy of Toyota

Page viii: Photo courtesy of General Motors

Page ix: Photo courtesy of Honda

Page x: Photo courtesy of Toyota

Page 1-3: Photo courtesy of Toyota

Page 6: Photo courtesy of Honda

Page 9: Photo of System Lohner-Porsche courtesy of Porsche Cars North America

Page 9: Photo of Woods Dual Power courtesy of Petersen Automotive Museum

Pages 11-12: Photo courtesy of Nancy Rogers

Page 23: Photo courtesy of Honda

Pages 29-30: Photos courtesy of Toyota

Page 36: Photo courtesy of Toyota

Page 37: Photo courtesy of Honda

Pages 38-59 Photo courtesy of Toyota

Pages 60-73: Photos courtesy of Honda

Pages: 74-81: Photos courtesy of Ford

Page 82-91: Photo courtesy of General Motors

Page 94: Photo courtesy of Hyundai

Page 100: Photo courtesy of Toyota

Page 102: Photo courtesy of BMW

Page 106-107: Photos courtesy of www.calcars.org

Page 114-117: Photos courtesy of Honda

Pages 118-119: Photos courtesy of Commuter Cars Corporation

Page 120: Photos courtesy of General Motors

Page 121: Photos courtesy of DaimlerChrysler

Page 122: Photos courtesy of Honda

Page 123: Photo courtesy of Hyundai

Page 124: Photo courtesy of Kia

Page 125: Photo courtesy of Nissan

Page 126: Photo courtesy of Suzuki

Page 127: Photo courtesy of Toyota

Page 129: Photo courtesy of www.Penn-Partners.org

Page 131: Photo courtesy of Accelerated Composites

{Index}

hybrid technology, 3, *32,* 32–33

hydrogen technology, 113–114

steam-powered technology, 102, *102*

Boulerie, Jean Charles, 132

Brabec, Filip G., 103

buses, diesel-electric, 33

Bush, George W., 2, 3

buyer demographics, 22, 24

C

Cadillac Escalade, 97

CAFE (Corporate Average Fuel Economy), 111

California Cars Initiative, 2–3, 22, 107

Cappa, Nicholas, 98

Car and Driver (magazine), 13

carbon dioxide, 15

carbon monoxide, 15

carburetors, 200-mile-per-gallon, 10

catalytic converters, 15

cellulosic ethanol, 112

Chevrolet Aveo, 120, *120*

Chevrolet Malibu, 97

Chevrolet Silverado Hybrid

production and specifications, 82, *84,* 84–87, *85, 87*

sales statistics, 13c

tax credits for, 20c

Chevrolet Tahoe, 97

Chrysler, 98

Chung, Mike, 16, 19

cities and hybrid popularity, 24

Clean Car Incentive Program, 14

Clooney, George, 21, 118, *118*

Commuter Cars Corporation, *118,* 118–119, *119*

compact cars, 119–127, *121–127*

company incentives, 19, 21

Consumer Reports (magazine), 16

continuous variable transmission, 34–35, *35,* 57, *67*

Corporate Average Fuel Economy (CAFE), 111

D

Daewoo, 120, *120,* 126, *126*

DaimierChrysler

future developments, 3, *32,* 32–33, 98, 108

I

J

K

L